NYMPHING
STRATEGIES

NYMPHING STRATEGIES

LARRY TULLIS

Preface by John Randolph

THE LYONS PRESS

Guilford, Connecticut
An imprint of The Globe Pequot Press

The Lyons Press is an imprint of The Globe Pequot Press.

Cover photograph by Tim Irwin.
Other photography by R. Valentine Atkinson/Frontiers (page 33), Dave Hughes (page 18), Tom Montgomery (page 70), Larry Tullis (pages 2 and 48), Egmont Van Dyck (pages120, 132/133).

Illustrations by Rod Walinchus.
FRONTISPIECE: *Carlos Muñoz at Paloma Lodge, Caihaique, Chile.*

Printed in the United States of America

10 9 8 7 6 5 4 3 2

The Library of Congress Cataloging-in-Publication Data is available on file.

CONTENTS

PREFACE

The most difficult task I ever undertook in the sport of fly fishing was learning how to fish the fly down. For several decades nymphs and wets were my fly-fishing downfall, until one bright morning on Nelson's Spring Creek in Montana.

I was fishing with my 12-year-old son and George Anderson, owner of the Yellowstone Angler in Livingston. George recommended that my son, a newcomer to nymphing, try a strike indicator, what we might call a bobber in another style of fishing. He tied on a tuft of yarn, greased it, and attached a Peeking Caddis nymph of his design, and my son made his first cast to a rising trout and caught it. Then my son went off on his own and we listened to his success as squeals of delight floated upriver from where he fished.

Strike indicators have been used for centuries, since Dame Juliana Berners provided our first instructions in the fifteenth century. They allow us to detect the strike before the fish can eject our fly. Quite simply, they allow novices to nymph successfully. Indicator fishing is the most basic form of nymph and wet-fly fishing. It provides us with an essential element of success: the means of achieving a drag-free drift *beneath the water.* This simple technique unlocks the first door to fly-fishing. It provides a foundation for learning other important techniques that can provide a lifetime of challenges and fulfillment, on species of fish as varied as Atlantic salmon, steelhead, panfish, and bass. We all can go beyond our successes with indicators to highly sophisticated line manipulations, weighting techniques, and special fly designs. But essentially we all come back to drag-free drift, and its modifications, as our founding principle.

Every angler needs help, and my son, luckily, got the right instruction from the right fly fisher. Would that I had had the same instruction at age 12.

This book provides that right insider information from the right fly fisher. This is the best and the most thorough nymphing and wet-fly instruction that I have seen in print. I have successfully used many of the techniques that the author describes; yet I have learned a great deal that is new from these pages, despite my 50 years of fishing, both as an amateur and as a professional.

Larry Tullis understands the instincts of trout and their survival behavior as well as any fly fisher who has dared to write about it. He provides his wisdom to us. He does not display knowledge; he shares it. This is his treasure-trove of nymphing lore revealed.

John Randolph
Harrisburg, Pennsylvania

INTRODUCTION

A rainbow trout this large would stir the heart of any angler, no matter how experienced. I was no exception. It hovered near the gravel drop-off. The rising waters from tailwater dam releases on the Green River in Utah created a smorgasbord. A dozen-plus good-sized trout darted back and forth as a banquet was swept off the bottom rocks and vegetation of a riffle, over the edge of the gravel bar. The large fish dwarfed the others and was feeding with an abandon seldom seen in fish of this dimension.

I knew I could catch some of these trout but I wanted to hook the big one. Since the water was fairly shallow, I adjusted the small strike indicator so it was only four feet from the fly. With a head still light from the adrenaline rush at the first sight of this tremendous fish, and hands that wouldn't quit shaking, I tied on an olive scud pattern, the fly of choice this time of the spring. A micro split-shot above the fly gave it enough weight.

The initial cast was placed about 10 feet upstream from the concentration of trout. This first cast is always the most important, so I was fully keyed in. It was short of the large fish, unfortunately, but a good-sized cutthroat trout darted over and nailed the fly, pulling the strike indicator under the surface. The hook was set and the fight was on. I instantly angled the rod downstream and waded toward shore to get this fish away from the feeding pod and avoid spooking the rest of the trout. The tactic worked and a beautiful 20-inch, Snake River finespot-strain cutthroat was landed.

I waded back into position and was soon into another fish, this time an acrobatic rainbow of 16 inches. I wanted to see what the fish were feeding on, so out came the stomach pump. The sample showed a selection of scuds, a couple of trout eggs, and a few mayfly nymphs. The fish were still feeding well so I waded quietly back and took the time to switch to a #16 light pink scud like one in the stomach sample. Two casts later, a feisty rainbow of 14 inches was caught and landed.

Several more casts landed right by my dream trout. The fish seemed to swerve over and almost touch the scud imitation twice, but the indicator never moved. I switched to a natural mayfly-nymph imitation and caught and released two more rainbow trout (19 and 17 inches) in the next 20 minutes, but the larger trout always managed to avoid my best presentations even though it was still feeding. An egg imitation caught another of the pack. I wondered what would take that big fish and stopped to analyze the situation. I had tried about eight different scud, mayfly, and egg patterns with good success but hadn't yet caught my prime target.

Looking down into the clear water at my feet, I saw moss drifting in the slowly rising waters. Suddenly something else crossed the toe of my shoe, something that looked like a caterpillar. I realized that it was a cranefly larva. Jackpot. I had been experimenting with cranefly-larva patterns the previous spring and still had a few tucked away in my boxes. So I tied on a natural-looking imitation and also changed the red strike indicator to a smaller white one. It would be harder to see but would be camouflaged in the surface foam in case the fish was onto my tricks.

My first cast was a little short so I wasn't mentally prepared when the large trout swerved over and smashed the cranefly. I nearly popped the fly off on the strike, but the knot held. The strike sank the hook home and the fish went ballistic, jumping straight toward me, giving me a good soaking and a second dose of adrenaline. It was one of the huge hybrid cuttbows, known on the Green River for their incredible fight. This one would go at least 12 pounds. In half a second it was jumping again out in the center of the run and then tail-walking upstream as the slack line became a tight line on a screaming reel.

The huge hybrid turned and headed straight downstream on a blazing run that threatened to break the tippet just from water tension. By the time I realized the fish was not going to turn, and I'd waded to shore and begun to follow, the trout was already in the rapids downstream and I couldn't even see the end of the fly line, just the white backing. I don't think an Olympic sprinter would have kept up with that fish, which was soon gone. The slack line indicated a broken tippet. I stood shocked for a moment, then smiled. As usual, my biggest fish of the day got away from me, and I didn't really mind. It had taken me 1 1/2 hours to hook the fish, but I had finally done it, and that was my real goal.

I sat down, reeled in the line, and rebuilt the leader sawed in half on a mid-river boulder. I went back up to the productive drop-off and caught three more trout that had moved in.

Besides being a very memorable experience, it was an enlightening one because I used to think that some fish were just too smart to be caught, and the fish I caught were just stupid. That experience 13 years ago got me thinking that all feeding trout in a general area could be caught, and that nymphs were the way to catch them much of the time.

Nymphing is a sometimes elegant and sometimes brutish way to fly fish. It has a history of over a hundred years in angling literature. Only recently have modern ideas and techniques really harnessed the potential of nymphing.

It's generally believed that stream trout feed mostly but not exclusively on nymphs and other subsurface critters. During typical summer aquatic insect hatches that may be true, but my observations suggest that some fish never feed on the surface. In winter or quiet seasons, a lack of dry-fly action makes all the fish feed subsurface all the time. And large trout seldom feed on top. Even during a mayfly, caddis, or midge hatch, many trout are nearly full on nymphs before they even consider feeding on the surface.

Once I was aware of this, I began to concentrate on various nymphing techniques and patterns, and had much more consistent success. I love good dry-fly action as much as anyone else, but I've discovered a love for applying the skills and finesse required to catch trout on nymphs. It takes more skill to become a good nymph angler than it does to become a good dry-fly fisherman, and nymphers are likely to catch many more fish as well. An incentive to learn.

NYMPHING DEFINED

The generic term "nymphing" requires explanation because nymphing can be done with non-nymph imitations. In this book, "nymphing" refers to fishing any subsurface, nymph-like imitation or any fly that is "nymphed." Since I want to cover all bases, I will consider subsurface insects and imitations plus other free-floating, subsurface foods and imitations, such as scuds, sow bugs, aquatic worms, fish eggs, snails, and leeches. The book will also include a small section on streamers, which can be nymphed and can sometimes simulate the larger nymphs as well.

Nymphing techniques are incredibly varied, but they are all designed to present the nymphs in a natural or attractive manner to the trout. No single technique works everywhere so I'll go over both popular and new techniques for nymphing. Experimentation is a key to success, but experiments without a purpose in mind are inefficient.

NYMPH IMITATIONS

The flies that are used in nymphing have recently undergone a metamorphosis of sorts, as has the philosophy of imitation. "Matching the hatch" is not the exact science many people think it is, and there are many other ways to trigger feeding, such as fishing suggestive flies, attractors, or hybrids, or using particular presentation techniques. To choose suitable fly patterns, the angler needs to understand the reasons why fish take certain types of fly patterns. This is far more useful than just being told exactly what fly to use.

OPPORTUNISTIC DRIFT

Most fly fishermen have heard that trout feed subsurface 90 percent of the time and on the surface 10 percent of the time, but few have translated those figures to actual fishing conditions. Every day there is at least one regular insect drift, which gets the fish feeding heavily well before a major hatch and even when there is no hatch. Some trout are already full by the time the adult insects are ready to be fed on. Those anglers who ignore nymphing opportunities not only ignore 90 percent of the fish's feeding habits but they also miss out on any opportunity to catch certain fish, often very large trout, that rarely, if ever, feed on the surface.

CROSSOVER APPLICATIONS

Nymphing has been redefined from the early days, and I'll explain some of the evolution that has affected the way we fish today. We use nymphing techniques to fish non-nymph imitations, and we fish nymph imitations by non-traditional methods. Both have become very big parts of modern nymphing. New ways of rigging have made nymphing an infinitely variable and effective endeavor, often crossing over into other types of fishing.

I recall one day many years ago when I was nymphing the famous Barns holes of the Madison River in Yellowstone Park. The action was slow except for the occasional whitefish and one rainbow. An angler fishing streamers below me hooked and landed a nice brown. I decided to try streamers but did not feel like re-rigging my strike-indicator nymphing system so I just substituted a streamer for the nymphs. I fished the streamer just as I did the nymphs, right along the bottom, and was quickly into several browns and rainbows. The other angler was impressed and came by to see what I was doing differently. I rigged him up the same way and demonstrated, and he was soon into several fish as well. In fact, he was doing better than I was. I watched him and discovered that he was not fishing an absolute natural drift. Instead, he had a little bit of tension on the line, and as he mended and twitched the line, the flies twitched and tumbled enticingly along the bottom. I changed my techniques as well, and we both had an embarrassingly fruitful day.

Remember that "nymphing" is not just fishing nymphs but is a technique that is suited to a variety of imitations. Most people fish ant patterns in the surface film. However, anglers who have fished sparsely tied imitations several inches below the surface, or even right along the bottom, know that they are often even more effective, especially in faster water areas. I encourage you to begin thinking laterally and creatively about nymphing.

Trout today get bombarded by so much of the same thing that when you present something different, or in just a slightly different way, they can't resist. Selective trout get keyed into rejecting traditional patterns and techniques, the "conditioned response," but they are also suckers for the new because they must be on the lookout constantly for additional food sources or new survival methods. Adaptability is what has made trout a success in so many waters worldwide.

NYMPHING OVERVIEW

This book will cover all the basic and advanced nymphing techniques. It does not cover some subjects already addressed in other volumes in Lefty's Little Library of Fly Fishing. Casting, for example, has already been covered quite well, but specialized nymphing presentation techniques will be included here.

You will learn how to collect trout foods in moving and stillwater, and how to relate those food items to the flies you choose. I don't believe you need to learn Latin just to imitate certain trout foods. Scientific names will not be used here. We will get into the life cycles of various foods, but more important, we will see how trout relate to each food or to each stage of the same food.

In the chapters that follow, you'll find out about the trout habits that affect trout feeding activity and why nymph feeding is the way selective trout deal with fishing pressure. Various species behave differently, and some are more susceptible to nymphing than others. I will show you how to deal with each species using nymphing techniques.

Trout are masters of their environment and can adapt to many situations, including angling pressure. They are often discriminating samplers that will reject commonly seen nymph patterns, especially nymphs with drag, but will sample just about anything else. This suggests that the angler should present fly patterns that the trout have not seen before. I will explain that presentation level and style are very important in nymphing. Another book in the Library, *Fly Fishing for Trout: Volume Two — Understanding Trout Behavior,* discusses the way trout see, but I will show how this relates to nymphing and how trout physiology and mentality affect the way they feed. For example, trout seldom grub the bottom; instead, they take free-floating items within their strike zone.

Perhaps the most important chapter in this book is the one entitled "Techniques and Rigging." Because most anglers do not rig or present the fly properly, presentation becomes a setback even if the right fly is used. Presentation accounts for 75 percent of your success rate. You'll learn the best nymphing rigs ever devised.

But the type of fly you choose is critical even though presentation is the most important. Selective trout can see flaws in presentation much more easily than they can see a fly pattern itself. Once they get close to the fly, however, clearer vision allows them to see the imitation more distinctly. Selective trout will quickly reject an improper imitation. Trout do not analyze everything; certain triggers let trout decide very quickly whether or not to take the fly. You will also learn how to choose nymphs for unfamiliar waters and how to read water type to determine which nymph types are most likely to produce the best.

Let's begin by taking a look at the wide variety of foods that drives trout nymphing activity.

OVERLEAF: *Western march brown nymph.*

CHAPTER ONE

THE NATURALS

The natural foods that trout feed on vary according to location. Each water type has its own set of critters designed to exist in that environment. When the nature of the river or lake changes, so does the variety of plant and animal life. You can learn how to look at a stream or lake and get a good idea about what kind of fly the trout will accept.

Each trout food looks and behaves differently and has differing stages of development. The trout know some basic things about their foods, such as the average sizes, where they normally see their foods, and how to intercept them. Let's start our discussion with the best way to become familiar with the trout foods on your angling waters.

COLLECTING TROUT FOODS

Nothing will teach you about nymphing faster than using a collection screen or a stomach pump (properly). Once you know the type of foods available, you already have a good idea what fly to use and which presentation technique is best. Most anglers don't bother with collection screens and end up spending the better part of their fishing day just blundering through their fly boxes hoping to stumble on a fly the fish want. Collection screens are most popular in rivers, but modified versions also work in lakes and ponds.

Collection Screens for Rivers

The basic collection screen for rivers is simply a section of window screen that is attached to two sticks. The sticks can be from one to four feet long, the screen a square that is slightly smaller than the length of each stick. Small collection screens are much more portable but suffer from having too small a collection surface. They are okay for small waters where you are collecting from the shallows, but they won't work in deeper water. Some commercial screens available have telescoping poles or are shock corded, tent-pole style, for easier storage.

The ideal collection screen is 1 1/2 to three feet wide and is attached to sticks three to four feet long. The easiest way to attach the screen material is simply to staple it to wooden rods, but you can get fancy and sew sleeves in the screen for the rods if you wish. Either way, make sure the rods extend about one inch below the screen. These nubs go down into the gravel or silt and help anchor the screen in the current.

Any screen material can be used, as long as the holes are not too large. I prefer a coated fiberglass screen. Some bridal-

River Collection Screen

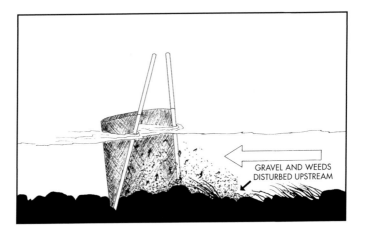

GRAVEL AND WEEDS
DISTURBED UPSTREAM

veil materials have smaller pores and can collect all sizes of insects. Window screen material will let the smallest immature midges and mayfly nymphs pass through but will stop insects and crustaceans about hook #22 or larger.

To use the assembled screen, place it quickly into the stream with the bottom spread wide. Firmly anchor the nubs with downward pressure and then bring the tops of the rods together so you can hold them with one hand. This reduces water pressure on the screen while allowing for maximum collection area. Disturb the bottom of the stream by digging in with one foot, raising rocks, or agitating weedbeds upcurrent from the screen. The dislodged aquatic critters will drift into the screen, and water pressure will hold most of them there. (Large stoneflies can crawl off fairly speedily.)

Pick the screen up out of the water without allowing the collection to be swept away. (This may take practice in fast water.) Walk to shore or to your boat and lay the screen out flat. The larger insects and other critters are seen fairly easily, but the smaller stuff may require getting down real close to the screen. A small, light-colored dish and delicate tweezers are helpful for placing the specimens in water for easier examination.

Notice first how many types of bugs are represented in the sample, then how many of each type. An abundance of one type of insect often means trout are also looking for that same type. Trout key in on the most abundant food item but are also open to other foods regularly seen. Notice everything. Is the stream heavily or lightly fished? I often bring a notebook to record the date, insect types, sizes, shapes, colors, locations, and river conditions for future reference.

Even more important, go through your nymph fly boxes and find the nymphs that come closest to the naturals. Note first the size. Is the imitation a little bigger or smaller than the naturals? Next compare the shape. Is the imitation too bulky or too skinny? Is the texture close enough to the naturals? A buggy nymph like the typical Gold-Ribbed Hare's Ear is a good imitation for the broad-shouldered nymphs of fast water but is not a good bet for slow, slick waters. A better imitation might be a Pheasant Tail Nymph.

If you think of some variations that would be closer to the naturals, make a note and tie some up next time you're near a tying kit. For example, you might observe a type of mayfly nymph with yellowish segmentations on a brown body. Your closest fly might have metallic gold ribbing for body segmentation, but a yellow thread ribbing might come much closer. Even if you don't tie your own flies, there is usually someone at a local fly shop who ties custom fly patterns for customers. As another example, nymphs about to change into adults often have a shiny bubble on their thorax or abdomen. The fly pattern variation would be a Flashback or Flashbutt Nymph, imitating this metallic sheen.

If your sample includes abundant larger nymphs, such as stoneflies, you probably got your sample from fast water, with bigger rocks around. If the bugs are predominantly hook #16 or smaller, you are most likely collecting in moderate or slow water. If there are lots of scuds, sow bugs, and leeches, you are likely on a spring creek or tailwater fishery.

Turn these statements around, and you will see that you can often tell what type of nymph pattern to start with just by looking at the water type. In fast water, your nymphs are going to be bigger, bulkier flies, #12 to #2. In moderate water, your nymphs will be medium-sized, #16 to #10 (unless the trout are catch-and-release conditioned, in which case you should use smaller flies). In slow water, your nymphs will be primarily sparsely tied #14 to #24 flies (with a few exceptions like brown, gray, or green drake mayflies). Every rule has its exceptions, but learning what type of nymph is in what type of water is a great place to start in choosing patterns, and nothing gives you more preliminary information than an insect collection screen.

Another method of determining which insects the trout are being exposed to is to leave the screen fully opened in the current (without disturbing the bottom) to catch the naturally drifting insects. It takes much longer, but it gives a more accurate indication of which bugs are most active and are therefore most available to the trout.

A variation of this technique is to hold the screen in the upper 12 inches of the current. You are then capturing only the nymphs preparing to emerge and the already emerged adults. It is intriguing to watch an insect metamorphose right before your eyes — from nymph or pupa to adult, winged insect. In fact, I've been known to completely forget about fishing for an hour or two while sampling.

I seldom keep screen samples, instead returning them to the water once I've made my notes. If you wish to preserve samples, have some small glass vials with corks handy. They should be pre-filled with a preserving fluid, available at many fly shops or scientific supply houses. I don't know of any fluid that keeps the bugs' natural colors for long, but you will at least have their size and shape for reference.

Collection Methods for Stillwater

For stillwater sampling, the lack of current requires a different collection method. You can often find rocks, submerged sticks, or clumps of vegetation near the shore that harbor nymphs and other foods. Use an aquarium net, or just grab a handful of something and set it on the screen for examination. A more accurate method is to build a small insect dredge that can be lowered to various depths for a more realistic sampling from trout feeding strata.

A child's cone-shaped, fine-mesh butterfly net can easily be modified to form a collection screen by removing the stick

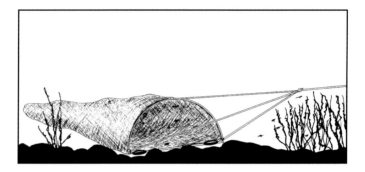

Lake Collection Screen

and bending the wire frame to a flat-bottomed shape (rectangle, half circle, or triangle). Tie three or four strings to the corners and weight the bottom corners with lead. Tie the corner strings to a main line and drop this gizmo from your float tube or boat. Let it sink to the bottom, then troll slowly in the area you're sampling. If it won't stay on the bottom, let out more line or add more weight. You can get fancy and put a "rake" on the front, at the bottom of the frame, to dislodge bottom dwelling insects in the silt. The rake is a necessity for sampling silt-dwelling mayflies but it is not needed for most bugs. Add a bottle to the end for easier sample viewing. The littoral zone (shallow, sunlit, weedy areas) will give you your best samples, but you should also try deeper waters.

Compare the naturals to your tied flies and make notes. Remember that you are only gathering information on the naturals and that exact imitation is not the only way to catch trout. (More on this later.) But using collecting screens is invaluable for learning about the waters you fish.

If minnows make up a large percentage of the trout's forage, you should use a minnow seine and then take photos or make quick observations and release the minnows unhurt. In some areas it is illegal to possess minnows, dead or alive.

Stomach Pumps

A stomach pump sounds bad, but if you use it properly it is reasonably safe to the trout and extremely educational for you. Once you catch a trout, the pump tells you exactly what that fish is feeding on. There is no guessing.

Use only stomach pumps from fly shops. If the suction is too strong, the tube too large, or the edges too sharp, a pump can damage the fish internally. The stomach pump should be used on trout only between 14 and 20 inches long. Smaller fish are easily damaged, and larger fish require the pump to be inserted too far down the gullet.

To use a stomach pump properly, first tire the trout sufficiently but not to exhaustion. Second, gently cradle the fish upside down, over or in the water, in one hand. Held in this way, the fish generally is calmed. (Never squeeze the trout.) Third, depress the bulb on the end of the pump and let the suction pull some river or lake water into the tube. Fourth, gently press the tube into the fish's gullet until you feel a slight resistance, which means you have reached the trout's food. You should never force the tube too far or too hard. Fifth, by gently squeezing the bulb, squirt half or a quarter of the water in the bulb into the trout's throat. The water will mix with the most recently eaten foods, and when you release pressure on the bulb, the suction will draw the water and food items back into the tube. Sixth, set the pump aside and concentrate on making sure the trout is well revived. Once the trout has been released, you can squirt the contents of the pump into your hand or into a small dish or your stripping apron (on float tubes) and examine.

If the fish you catch squirms around too much, or if the safety of the fish is in question, don't use the stomach pump. Wait for a more cooperative or more suitable fish. Avoid using the pump in water warmer than 65 degrees F. since warm water makes trout difficult to revive.

If you decide to use a collection device, please do so responsibly. Learn to use a stomach pump properly, and use it sparingly. Digging up too much of the stream bottom when preparing to collect with an insect screen can damage the biological seal. If you turn over a rock during sampling, turn it right-side up again.

Your collection kit should include the following items: collection screen, small metric ruler, sample dish, delicate fine-tip tweezers, stomach pump, notepad, pencil, Borger Color System match booklet (to correctly identify a critter's color for reference), collection vials with preserving fluid, and maybe a camera with a macro-focusing lens (for a photo file).

INSECTS ARE SHEEP

Now that you have an idea how to collect trout food in your fishing waters, let's learn some of the traits that make insects available to trout. You might ask, "Why don't insects just hide from the fish?"

The main reason is *natural drift*. Every day there occurs at least one insect movement or migration related to light intensity and grazing patterns. Grazing like sheep or cows, the insects feed on the rocks' slime layer and then move on to other, fresher pastures by drifting with the current or by swimming or walking. The drift is when the trout feed on them the most.

Each day this insect drift occurs, unseen by creatures on land. The trout are very interested, and this daily nymph migration triggers trout feeding activity even when no hatches are present. When light levels are low, as in winter or on overcast days, the natural drift might be concentrated in the middle of the day, from about 10:00 to 3:00. On a typical fishing day in summer, there are two distinct drifts: one in the morning, between 7:00 and 10:00, and another in the afternoon or evening. Does that mean that nymphing is not good midday? No, because trout are opportunistic, and some trout will be feeding at all hours. But you can experience some fantastic fishing if you key in on the periods of greatest natural drift and, therefore, the greatest nymphing opportunities. Trout often gorge themselves during these times and feed only selectively in between.

Hatches also make the insects available to the trout. Mayfly nymphs are slow swimmers. As they ascend the water column, they drift quite a distance before reaching the surface. Once they're up to the surface film, they take a while longer to break through it. The whole time, they are easy targets for the trout. The fish you see bulging the surface may actually be feeding subsurface. Caddis pupae are much faster swimmers than mayfly nymphs, so the trout must also be fast, and they will often take the emergers with a splashy rise. The rise form of the trout will often give you clues to which insect they're feeding on.

Hatch times are determined by many factors and are not always easy to predict. Some insects prefer sunny days and others hatch almost exclusively on cloudy, rainy days. Water temperature, light intensity, runoff stage, water chemistry, season, water clarity, and stage of growth all affect the time of a hatch. Here again, most hatches occur midday when the light levels are low, and morning or evening when light levels are high in summer (with many notable exceptions). When the hatch is going strong and the fish are rising steadily, the best nymphing action has already come and gone. Ask locals when the hatch usually starts, and you know when to concentrate on the hatch drift — one to two hours earlier.

Nymphing addicts will continue to nymph even during a hatch, and they will do well, especially on the larger fish that rarely rise. Many anglers can't pass up the chance to cast dry flies to rising trout. However, once they've had some great hatch nymphing action, that might change. I get lots of satisfaction by starting with nymphs and crustacean imitations, then as the hatch begins, switching to ascending and emerging nymphs, then to adult dry flies. Following trout-feeding activity is very intriguing and keeps you busy changing fly patterns, leader rigs, and presentation techniques.

AQUATIC INSECTS

No nymph angler can consider himself competent until he has an understanding of how trout and aquatic insects are linked. This section of the book will help you learn about mayflies, caddisflies, stoneflies, midges, craneflies, damselflies, and dragonflies, and how trout relate to them. You can get as deep into entomology as you like elsewhere, but the following section sticks to just these basic insect groups.

Mayflies

Mayflies are imitated more than any other aquatic insect. They are elegant, easy to imitate, common in most trout streams, and they have a long literary history. The adults look like little sailboats on the water. They are found in many lakes and ponds but are most often fished in slow to moderately fast-current streams. Some anglers fish nothing but mayfly imitations on their favorite waters. They know about when the hatches are expected, and they fish those times. Summer evening mayfly hatches are fun to fish after work if a stream is close by, but remember there is also an evening drift of nymphs that can be fished right up to dark.

Mayfly-nymph imitations are tied on #8 to #24 hooks, #12 to #18 being used most often. They are usually light yellowish brown to shades of brown and olive, but there are hundreds of variations even in the same species. Mayfly nymphs molt their skins as they grow, and as they do, they become lighter in color and acquire the softer body that trout seem to like. Different water chemistry, insect foods, and the color of the surroundings contribute to nymph colors.

A mayfly nymph has a long, tapered abdomen and a thicker thorax. Fast-water mayfly nymphs are usually the broadest shouldered, and feature strong legs to cling to the rocks, and a quickly tapering body. Slow-water or stillwater nymphs are more delicate-looking, with a thinner, smoother body. Gills are located along the sides of the abdomen (big gills for slow water, small gills for fast water), and there are two or three tails. Mayfly nymphs may be swimmers, crawlers, clingers, or burrowers, depending on their species, their behavior, and the habitat they prefer.

Trout will feed opportunistically on mayfly nymphs any time of the day but go crazy during great nymph movements. The trout start feeding in the deeper runs and pools, but as the insects become more abundant, the trout seek out the source of the food, often in the very productive water of riffles. So at the height of the nymph drift, many trout will move into quite shallow water or along drop-offs to feed. Much of the fastest nymphing action I've seen takes place in less than two feet of water. The choppy surface masks the angler's movements, and trout feel relatively safe from predators. Simple nymphing techniques work, and the flies seldom need to be weighted with more than a micro split-shot. Three to 6-weight rods are usually sufficient.

When the trout are not in the shallows, you will need to fish deep in the good holding water below riffles and rapids. (More on this under "Nymphing Techniques.") Slick water is more difficult to nymph but very possible with the two-fly or greased-leader techniques described later. Because mayflies are slow swimmers, you should present the artificials naturally, with little if any movement.

Caddisflies

Caddisflies are much like aquatic moths. With their tent-shaped wings, the adults are often mistaken for moths, and the larvae look like grubs. Caddis are the second-most imitated aquatic insect of fly rodders. But there are far fewer dry-fly imitations for caddis than for mayflies, because one pattern in several sizes or colors can cover many individual species.

The nymphs are a different story. All caddis larvae look like grubs, but they come in many colors, from bright insect green and olive to tan to almost pure white. They have dark heads and short legs. Many species build cases of sand, sticks, or organic debris for protection. Some spin nets on rocks, making insect hammocks. Caddis larvae come in many sizes, from hook #6 to #24, but most are in the #12 to #18 range. They are hardier than many mayflies, so they are more important for fish in warmer water or in water of poorer quality.

When caddis larvae get ready to hatch, they change into a pupal stage, which is also grub-like, but with wing pads and long legs for fast swimming. Many of the old-style wet flies imitated this stage. Swinging these patterns in the current imitates the fast-swimming pupae. Most caddis species hatch during the summer, a few in the spring or fall.

Trout will feed on the larvae any time of the year if available. The larvae are poor swimmers and are easy prey if dislodged and drifting. The pupal stage is imitated with patterns different from the larval stage, even in the same species. Pupae are more translucent and often have shiny bubbles to help them ascend to the surface faster. Larva imitations are fished natural-drift, and the pupae are often fished with some movement to imitate the swimming speed.

While caddis are sometimes fished in slow or stillwater, the naturals are most often associated with riffles and pocket water. Many fast-water streams in the U.S. have prolific caddis populations, but most trout streams have caddis in some numbers.

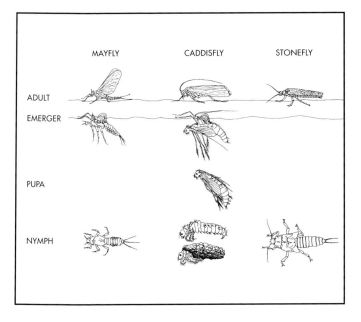

	MAYFLY	CADDISFLY	STONEFLY

Mayfly, Caddisfly, and Stonefly Life-Cycle Stages

If there are many cased caddis or grub-like, free-roaming caddis in your screening sample or under submerged rocks and branches, you can be certain that the trout are feeding on them as well. Some stillwaters have good caddis populations, so the pupal and adult imitations are effective, especially when they are fished in high-elevation waters.

Stoneflies

There's something of a mystique surrounding stoneflies. The relatively large size of some species makes trout take notice, especially very large trout. I think more really big river trout have been caught on imitations of stoneflies than on imitations of any other order of insects. Stoneflies don't exist in all streams. They need fast, well-oxygenated, clean water.

Slow water or poor-quality water is unacceptable to them. They are not found in stillwater unless there is a fast current or spring flowing in close by. The insects are sometimes found in moderate currents in springs, and below fastwater stretches.

Small stonefly nymphs are often mistaken for mayfly nymphs. The difference between them is fairly obvious up close. Stonefly nymphs have their gills under the thorax rather than along the abdomen, and they always have two tails, never three like some mayflies. Typical mayfly-nymph patterns imitate small stonefly nymphs just fine, but the larger stonefly nymphs require specific patterns. Large stonefly nymphs can be 1/2 inch to three inches long and range from a creamy yellow to brown to black. Because of the nymphs' size, trout cannot ignore them as a food source. One large stonefly might be equivalent to a hundred small mayfly nymphs.

If the water you're to fish is clean and fast, such as rapids, pocket water, or boulder-filled riffles, start with a stonefly pattern. And if it's big trout you're after, tie on a stonefly nymph and move up into the faster runs. Exact imitations are usually not called for because of the fast water, but the size and shape of the fly should be a good simulation of the natural. Typical stonefly nymph imitations are tied on #10 to #1 hooks. Smaller nymphs are imitated with standard mayfly-nymph patterns or with attractors.

Stoneflies have a life cycle similar to that of mayflies, but there is no emerger stage for the fisherman to imitate because stoneflies migrate to shore and crawl up on streamside vegetation to hatch, instead of swimming to the surface. The bigger species have a three to five-year life cycle, so they are always available to trout. After the bigger nymphs hatch, there are still two or three sizes for trout to feed on. Stoneflies are poor swimmers and will often curl up while drifting in the cur-

Fishing the Fall River in Northern California. ➤

rent, so many imitations are tied on curved hooks or are bent after tying. They are fished natural-drift, along the bottom, often heavily weighted to get down in the fast, deep runs where big trout lurk. The large, weighted nymphs often require a 5 to 7-weight rod and line to cast them.

Midges

Midges are the most prolific insects in many streams and are often overlooked by anglers because of their small size. Midge larvae seldom reach 1/2 inch and most are less than 1/4 inch and slender. They are important to trout because of their numbers and because of their availability when other insects are scarce, such as in winter and early spring. They are often very important to lake and pond trout, especially when the insects hatch in incredible numbers during the spring. Stream midges are usually small, but stillwater varieties can get over 1/2 inch long.

Midges sometimes lay eggs two or more times a year. Some waters have midge hatches almost every day. The trout will feed on other insects when a larger or more abundant insect is readily available, but on a year-round basis, midges are found in stomach samples more than any other insect. That makes them important to nymphers and dry-flyers alike. Midges can often be fished throughout the year with excellent success.

Their life cycle is very much like a mosquito's, but luckily they don't bite. The segmented, worm-like larva has a small, dark head and is a slow but active swimmer, often called a little wiggler. Some species can elongate like a leech; the red midge larvae are called bloodworms and trout sometimes look for them. The wiggling action is almost impossible to imitate, so the best presentation technique is generally a natural drift in streams or a very slow retrieve in lakes. The pupa swims to the surface and hangs there suspended vertically in the surface film until the adult can emerge. Clusters of these pupae

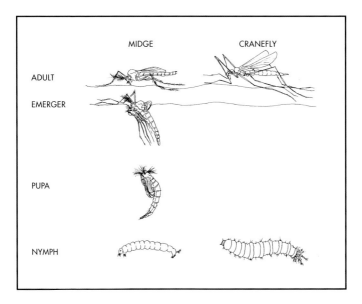

Midge and Cranefly Life-Cycle Stages

and adults often raft together, and trout will take several in one mouthful. The larvae are fished singly. Flies range from #8 to #28, average sizes being #14 to #24. Midge enthusiasts often use 1 to 5-weight rods for a delicate touch with the small hooks and light leaders, even on large trout.

Craneflies

Craneflies are very similar to midges, but some species are quite large, up to four inches long. The adults are those bugs that fly around your camp lantern and look like giant mosquitos (but don't bite). The smaller species are almost indistinguishable from midges and are fished in the same way. The larger varieties are poor swimmers and have only short nubs for legs. They look like underwater caterpillars, with a small, dark head and a watery olive, tan, gray, or rust-colored body.

Although they are widely distributed insects, craneflies are not available to the trout very often — mostly when rising waters in the spring or tailwater releases from a dam wash them loose from underwater muck or gravel or streamside decaying leaves. When they are available, however, big trout can become interested. A screen sample or stomach pump is the best way to find out if they are around. Cranefly patterns are also worth a try if you see some of the adults skimming the water's surface in the spring.

They are fished natural-drift in the current and are most commonly imitated on #8 to #2 hooks. The smaller craneflies are fished just like midges. My best luck on cranefly larvae has been in deep, swift runs and on the drop-offs below mixed weed and gravel-bar areas.

Damselflies

Damselflies are found in many stillwater environments and also in some slower streams. The adults are the flies that look like skinny dragonflies, often bright blue in color. The nymphs are usually olive or brown and live in the aquatic vegetation of lakes, ponds, and sloughs. Their long, thin, delicate body distinguishes them from dragonfly nymphs. They have long, thin legs, and three paddle-like tails which help them swim, slowly and with lots of serpentine wiggle.

Trout feed on all sizes of these insects when they are available, but they especially key in to the large migrations that occur mid-summer as the nymphs prepare to hatch. The nymphs ascend to the surface where they swim until they reach some vegetation or other structure extending above the water. There they climb out and hatch into adults. If you're float tubing, they will often climb onto your tube and hatch. They are easy to intercept, and the trout gorge themselves with abandon. It can be the fastest stillwater fishing you've ever witnessed, or the fish might get gorged and make fishing slow.

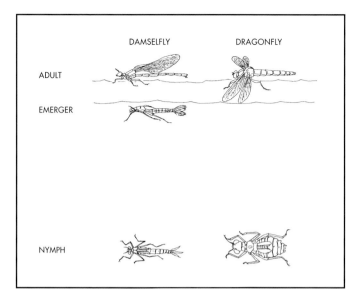

Damselfly and Dragonfly Life-Cycle Stages

Imitations are fished deep and slow until the beginning of the migration, at which point they are fished slow and shallow. Most commercially available fly patterns are olive-colored and have marabou or soft dubbing to imitate insect movement. They are tied on #12 to #6 hooks.

Dragonflies

Dragonflies are closely related to damselflies but in physical appearance are as different as damsels are from dragons. They also exist mostly in stillwaters and sloughs. The adults are much bigger than damselfly adults, and the nymphs are fat and chunky (and they can bite). The nymphs are oval-shaped with two distinct body segments, the abdomen being thicker. Dragonfly nymphs often propel themselves by squirting jets of water through their body.

They are fished weighted in short, fast strips to imitate the erratic swimming motion of the naturals. Imitations generally sport two body sections and soft hackle for legs. Patterns have two tails and are colored in shades of brown and green. Because the nymphs are 1/2 inch to two inches long and fat, they represent a large food item to trout and are opportunistically taken where familiar. Trout hit them hard, probably trying to kill them on the strike to avoid being bitten.

Because dragonflies are generally the largest insects in stillwater, large trout look for them in addition to their other meals of minnows, leeches, and crustaceans. Imitations are most often tied on #10 to #4 hooks. The insects are available to trout in the aquatic vegetation, and imitations are often fished in the channels between weedbeds.

OTHER SUBSURFACE TROUT FOODS

Aquatic insects are only part of the trout's food. Some nymphing patterns do not imitate true insect nymphs although they are fished in the same way and can sometimes be interchanged for true nymph patterns. Trout in some waters such as spring creeks, eutrophic lakes, and tailwater fisheries rely heavily on scuds, sow bugs, or crayfish. Patterns of other foods of importance, including aquatic and terrestrial worms, fish eggs, snails, pancora crabs, minnows, and salmon flesh, can all be fished exactly as you would true nymph patterns. Even patterns for terrestrial insects, like ants and beetles, can be nymphed, because terrestrials are frequently swept underwater.

Too often, anglers focus on imitating just the main four aquatic insect orders and family (mayflies, caddisflies, stoneflies, and midges). Trout in well-fished areas are likely to key on foods that are "safe" to eat. Since most nymphers use the Big Four imitations, safe foods are often the other foods discussed below. I call this category "trout junk food," when in reality it might be more nutritious than the usual foods.

Scuds and Sow Bugs

Wherever scuds and sow bugs are common, so are fat, fast-growing trout. Many tailwater streams and spring creeks are full of these active crustaceans. Scuds are sometimes the main trout food in tailwaters or some stillwaters where insect diversity or biomass is low. Since they do not hatch like insects, they are always available to trout.

Scuds are small, shrimp-like critters that swim using their legs or flippered tail. The body is segmented, and they have antennae. Scuds are tied on #6 to #26 hooks, and the average is #12 to #18. Common scud colors are olive, tan, pink, amber, and gray. Scuds are translucent, so most imitations are tied with translucent dubbing materials. Dead scuds turn orange because of the carotene in their system; stomach-pump samples are often orange or amber-colored. Many scud imitations are tied on curved hooks, which is not always accurate. A dead scud in your hand is curled up, but a live, swimming model is almost straight and I believe is best imitated with only a slight curve, if any. Orange scuds are often taken for drifting fish eggs as well.

Sow bugs are very similar to scuds in size and share the same habitat, but they have a wide, flat body that makes them look a lot like an aquatic potato bug. Sow-bug patterns are often interchangeable, especially with suggestive scud patterns. Colors are not as variable, usually ranging from a blue gray to a grayish brown, with occasional olives. They are heavily segmented.

Both scuds and sow bugs are fished natural-drift in most streams but can be swung up at the end of the drift. This illusion of a quickly swimming scud sometimes triggers strikes,

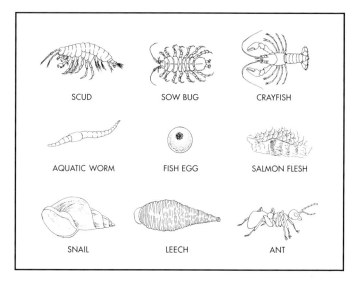

Trout Junk Food

but the patterns really are best fished naturally. In stillwater, the retrieve is slow but erratic.

Crayfish

Another crustacean is the crayfish, or crawdad. It looks like a mini-lobster and is more often associated with bass lakes than with trout waters. Big trout love crayfish, and they often exist together, in lakes and some streams. Even small trout can feed on the smaller crayfish and the soft-shell stages. Crayfish-feeding trout grow big and mean, having done battle with an armored prey having pincers for weapons and capable of swimming backwards by flipping its tail under its body.

Crayfish are 1/2 inch to over six inches long, so they represent a large food source trout can't ignore — if they can deal with the crayfish's defenses. Big browns, rainbows, brookies, and lakers are likely to take notice of crayfish.

The imitation can be as simple as a brown Woolly Bugger, which also imitates dragonfly nymphs quite well. Crayfish imitations are commonly tied on #10 to #1/0 hooks. Trout seem to prefer the #4 to #8 range.

Fishing these large morsels in stillwater is the same as fishing dragonfly nymphs — deep and moderately fast. Make the pattern look like an escaping food moving along muddy bottoms with rocks. In streams, I've found a natural drift is better, just as it is for a big nymph.

Daphnia

Daphnia are small crustaceans, like micro-scuds, barely visible to the naked eye, which makes them virtually impossible to imitate singly. Luckily, they school up in colonies in many lakes and reservoirs, and a cluster of daphnia can be imitated with some of the variegated-leech yarn flies available, such as the #10 to #4 Canadian Brown Leech. The spectrumized, fuzzy, translucent yarn triggers a feeding action from daphnia-feeding trout. Stomach samples have proven this to me in many lakes where they coexist. It is an overlooked food that deserves more attention from trouters.

Remember the biggest animal that swims, the blue whale, also feeds on these micro-edibles. Big trout can grow large while feeding mainly on daphnia and are often never hooked by anglers fishing more standard lake patterns. Trout swim through clouds of these foods with their mouth open, and their gills help strain the protein-rich foods into their gullet. Other fish just gulp mouthfuls whenever a concentration is found. The flies can be fished on the sink, with no action or on a slow retrieve with occasional pauses.

Aquatic Worms

Commonly called "San Juan Worms" by fly rodders, aquatic worms often resemble terrestrial redworms, and they live in the aquatic substrate of tailwater fisheries and spring creeks. They are taken by scud-eating trout as well because they are frequently available at the same times and places. Scuds and aquatic worms can be seen any time of the year, so trout learn to be opportunistic on them. Even selective trout often pounce on a San Juan Worm when it comes by. Aquatic worms are especially sought after when tailwater dam releases cause waters to rise quickly, washing many worms loose. Trout will line up at drop-offs to intercept the drifting smorgasbord. Much moss or turbidity can accompany such a water release, and San Juan Worms are easily seen, even in murky water.

The natural worms can range from 1/2 inch to four inches long, and other less available varieties might get much bigger. (Night crawlers can be four to eight inches long.) Aquatic redworms are commonly 1/16 to 1/8 inch thick and reddish or pinkish tan. Some are rust, gray, or brown. Imitations are usually tied on a #12 to #8 hook with lengths of the body extending front and back. Ultra-chenille is a common body material. Dyed, red glove leather works quite well and becomes softer when wet. Yarns and plastic strands are also used.

The worms cannot swim fast and can elongate like a leech. In streams, fish the pattern natural-drift and let the current produce the twisting action of the natural.

Fish Eggs

The most controversial trout food is fish eggs. Not long ago, any imitations of eggs or egg clusters were disguised as salmon and steelhead-type wet flies. Single-egg imitations got a slow start because many anglers considered them similar to bait. It took Alaska's remarkable rainbow and char fisheries to change attitudes towards egg patterns.

In Alaska, trout feed on the loose salmon eggs drifting from spawning fish. They grow extremely fast and are very energetic, and some trout take nothing else when keyed in on eggs.

Once egg fishing became accepted in Alaska, it began to be accepted elsewhere, and now egg fishing is common in many trout waters. Trout spawn in the spring or fall, and suckers and whitefish also spawn, creating numbers of drifting eggs. Some fish will ignore all else. There are times and places when you must imitate eggs to catch certain fish.

There are ethics questions about fishing spawning areas. Catching fish around spawning areas does little if any damage if the fish are played quickly and released properly. Spawning fish go right back to spawning, and most of the fish caught are there to feed, not spawn. Most damaging is walking on spawning beds, which crushes hundreds of eggs. Whether you decide to fish to spawn-eating trout or not, you must learn to recognize the clean gravel depressions and mounds of spawning redds so that you can avoid walking on them. Many of the same people who condemn spawning-bed anglers unknowingly stand or walk on beds and end up doing much more damage. If angling during spawning is found to be detrimental, then the seasons should be adjusted accordingly.

Experienced egg anglers can have some remarkable action. Eggs are fished natural-drift along the stream bottom like nymphs, although some aggressive fish will hit a swinging egg pattern or even one that is stripped like a streamer. Imitations are made from yarns, chenilles, beads, or dubbing. Orange, amber, or pink scuds are often taken for eggs by trout. Attractor eggs can be any bright color from chartreuse to fluorescent fuchsia. Fresh, natural eggs are often translucent and bright orange, amber, or reddish orange. As the eggs get bleached by the water or the sun, they become peachy or pinkish and more opaque. Egg anglers know the color of the eggs available and imitate it as closely as possible. Egg color is often more important than size, but selective egg feeders do also key in on size — four to 10 millimeters in diameter, five to six millimeters on average.

I guided Alaska for several years, and some of my most intriguing fishing was sight-nymphing for large egg-feeding rainbows in the clear streams of the Iliamna region. I think fly fishing includes fishing imitations of all foods trout feed on, and eggs are definitely one of them. Some of the dumbest feeders I've encountered, as well as some of the most selective, have been egg feeders, which keeps things interesting.

Salmon Flesh

On Alaskan salmon streams, at the end of the spawning season, the dead salmon start to decay and are torn apart by the rocks and logs in the rivers. The trout feed heavily on the pieces of salmon flesh drifting in the current, a last big feast before the long winter. It sounds unappetizing, but just think of it as salmon jerky for trout.

Flesh flies can catch some of the biggest Alaskan rainbows of the season (late August through November), so they are fished quite often. White, tan, or peach Bunny Bugs or tow-yarn streamers are fished natural-drift just like the eggs, or on a slow swing. Large Bunny Bugs (two to five inches long) are good for fast streams where big chunks of flesh tear loose from salmon in the current. Small sizes are better in many streams where slower currents just roll the salmon along the bottom, making small fragments of flesh more common. Cast to areas where you see salmon carcasses in the current, because the trout are often just downstream.

Snails

Snails are fed on by trout in lakes and streams. Some trout get keyed in on them and eat so many that their bellies become crunchy with the shells. The snails are sometimes taken right from the vegetation they are climbing on, but are more often eaten as they float suspended in the current or slowly rise to the surface with a bubble of air. If you see floating snails on the water or catch a trout whose stomach is crunchy, you can be sure the trout are feeding on snails.

Snails range from light tan to dark olive brown. Imitations are simply balls of similarly colored dubbing on a wide-gape hook, or peacock-body nymphs with soft brown hackle. The snail pattern is fished natural-drift in streams. In lakes, strip the fly once or twice, then let it sit for two to 30 seconds before stripping it again. The strip catches the trout's attention; hits usually come on the hesitation.

Minnows

It might seem strange to talk about minnows in a book about nymphing, but many nymph imitations are taken by the trout for minnows and vice versa. When streamers are fished in lakes, they might also be imitating dragonfly nymphs or crayfish at the same time. Some patterns such as the Woolly Bugger make no distinction, and the trout will take them for nymphs, minnows, leeches, or crayfish. In streams, you can fish streamers as you would natural-drift a nymph — right along the bottom, with the current, and using a strike indicator. Even streamers fished on the swing might be taken for nymphs ascending to the surface.

We might think we know what we are imitating, but trout often have different ideas, which is why suggestive flies often outperform exact imitations. Suggestives leave the interpretation to the trout rather than force-feeding it something specific. Nearly all fly patterns can be taken for something other than their intended forms. A Woolly Bugger works almost everywhere because it simulates so many things, like a minnow, leech, dragonfly nymph, damselfly nymph, stonefly nymph, crayfish, cranefly larva, or an aquatic worm.

Try to keep an open mind about patterns. Don't get locked into offering just one imitation of one food all the time. Leave some of the interpretation to the trout.

Leeches

Leeches are invertebrates that live in many stillwater and stream environments and often get placed in the nymph or streamer category. They are well known to trout because of their relative size and food value. A leech is a flattish worm that can elongate and that swims in a smooth up-and-down motion. Sometimes it also drifts with the current in streams, and a trout can intercept it just as it does other natural-drift foods. Leeches are sometimes mottled, sometimes flat-colored. Black is a common imitation color, but browns, olives, tans, and grays are often more accurate. Some are even purplish.

Leeches can be 1/2 inch to more than 12 inches long and are usually fished on long-shank #8 to #4 hooks. Weighted versions are common. As you strip the fly and pause, the fly will jig up and down somewhat, mimicking the undulations of the natural. Leech imitations are so free of details that trout may take them for minnows, nymphs, eels, or other foods. Some of my best big-trout days on reservoirs took place when I was fishing with leech-style flies.

Sunken Terrestrials

Land-dwelling insects are known as terrestrials. The floating versions of beetles, hoppers, and other terrestrials are often imitated, but few people fish them subsurface. However, trout in choppy water and back eddies look for terrestrial insects underwater. Ants, grasshoppers, cicadas, inchworms, and beetles all get swept into the current because of poor flying judgment, gusty breezes, rising water levels, or misplaced footing on overhanging streamside vegetation, or because they are dropped by birds.

Even adult, winged aquatic insects can be fished subsurface. Spent or unlucky adult stoneflies, mayflies, and caddis are often swept underwater and drowned. Therefore, the riffles or rapids below flat water and nearby drop-offs are good places to fish sunken adult insects. The imitations used are often referred to as "wet flies."

I remember one day on the Green River in Utah when I used a stomach pump to determine what the fish were feeding on. Most of the pump sample was made up of small mayfly nymphs and scuds, but there was also one small black ant. I thought that was unusual because this fish was obviously feeding along the bottom. After catching several trout in a riffle on mayfly-nymph and scud imitations, the action slowed. Just for fun, I switched to a black ant fished on my standard nymphing rig and was rewarded by several more trout. I've kept a few subsurface terrestrial imitations handy since then and have found them valuable hatch-busters for selective fish.

OVERLEAF: *A Chilean brown trout caught on a caddis pupa.*

CHAPTER TWO

THE TROUT

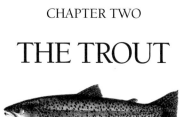

This chapter deals with some of the fascinating aspects of trout. Now that you know about some of the attributes of trout "nymphs," let's learn more about the trout and how they interact with their food and our flies. Each species of trout has characteristics that make it feed differently. Triggers for trout feeding activity are varied, and knowing them helps you get much more consistent fishing action than if you just match the nymph hatch or use what the fly shop recommends.

DIFFERENCES BETWEEN TROUT SPECIES

In fishing for all species of trout, I have noticed some distinct differences in how the individual species relate to their environment. There are nymphing possibilities for browns, rainbows, cutthroats, brookies, goldens, lakers, Arctic char, Dolly Varden, bull trout, anadromous trouts, grayling, and whitefish, but each species relates to its foods a little differently.

Brown Trout

Brown trout are the most widely distributed trout in the world, thanks to the British and others who stocked trout wherever they went. Browns can handle moderately warm water and marginal water quality better than other trout species, but they also thrive in prime trout waters. Scientists have determined that browns learn five times faster than rainbow trout, which allows browns to live in rivers that limit numbers of trout killed. As fishing pressure increases, they can adapt their feeding habits to avoid capture. Early on, they become more selective on dry flies, which most fly fishers use, and feed more heavily on nymphs or large foods that enable them to eat only occasionally.

Brown trout are very carnivorous and feed often on minnows and smaller trout. They also feed on nymphs and crustaceans. In fact, they have been known to eat anything they can fit into their mouth. A friend once used his boat net on a trout he saw thrashing on the surface. It turned out to be two 25-inch browns fighting over a 14-inch rainbow.

Browns jump regularly in cold water, not often in warmer waters. They are found in rivers but also adapt to some lake environments, and some strains, called "sea trout," are anadromous. River browns like the deeper runs below rapids and riffles but will venture into the shallows frequently and are often associated with structure — logs, undercut banks, rock ledges, overhanging brush, old car bodies, weedbeds, or drop-offs. In stillwater, look for browns on the deeper edges off weedbeds and near submerged, rocky shelves or at lake outlets. They will often feed shallow before first light and again after sunset. Browns are fall spawners.

Typical nymph-eating browns are six to 22 inches long. Bigger fish usually feed on minnows, crayfish, or other larger foods, but there are exceptions. A friend recently caught a 16-pound brown on a #16 scud on the Green River in Utah.

Rainbow Trout

Rainbows are popular worldwide because of their fighting ability, acrobatics, and catchability, and the ease with which they are raised in hatcheries. They love cool reservoirs and clean, fast, well-oxygenated waters. Steelhead are sea-run rainbows. Rainbows are mainly insect eaters but will prey on minnows and crayfish once they reach 16 to 30 inches or more.

"Bows" are often found in holding water of very fast water areas — in rapids and shallow riffles and behind boulders. They regularly feed in water six inches to three feet deep, especially in riffles and runs. Rainbows are much better fighters as native or naturalized hatchery fish; freshly planted rainbows are poor sport fish and generally undesirable to fly anglers. Lake rainbows regularly reach large sizes, yet still often feed on nymphs. If you want a big trout on a fly, there is nothing better than fishing nymph, leech, or crustacean imitations at a good, stillwater rainbow fishery.

Although they learn more slowly than browns, rainbows are ultra-selective in catch-and-release waters. Once hooked, they often get airborne, a beautiful sight. They interbreed with cutthroat trout and produce a hybrid known for its fighting ability. Rainbows are spring spawners.

Cutthroat Trout

Cutthroat trout are native to the western U.S. and Canada and have not been transplanted to many other parts of the world. Dozens of subspecies exist and are common in high-elevation waters near their ancestral homes. They do not compete well with introduced species and have therefore been pushed out of many waters. Because many of the waters that cutts still inhabit are pristine, solitary anglers like to fish for them. The fish are the dominant species in many western wilderness waters. Although they are most often associated with streams, there are a few notable stillwater cutthroat fisheries, such as Pyramid Lake, Henry's Lake, Strawberry Reservoir, and Yellowstone Lake.

Some subspecies of cutthroat are almost exclusively insect eaters. Others are highly predatory on minnows. Stream cutts fall for both dries and nymphs. Lake cutts feed mostly on the nymphs and scuds around weedbeds, springs, or inlets. The predatory cutts feed on minnows and large nymphs.

Cutthroat are generally considered the least intelligent of the trout species, but when they are caught-and-released frequently, they can become as selective as any other trout. Their fighting ability is less flashy, but they are good dog fighters. Cutthroat trout are spring spawners.

Brook Trout

Brook trout belong to the char family but are closer in habits to true trout because they are insect feeders as well as carnivores. They were originally found in the eastern U.S. and Canada but have become widely distributed in North America. Brookies prefer clean, cold waters, so they are common in high-elevation lakes and streams of the Rockies.

Brookies feed on just about anything they can fit into their gullet. They eat minnows when available but more often feed on insects and crustaceans. Stream brookies are usually small and often stunted, but in lakes brook trout can be large and chunky. Lake fish often congregate in areas like inlets and springs where they can feed on minnows, eggs, insects, and crustaceans. They are not considered very fast learners but can become selective in catch-and-release waters.

Streamers are the traditional flies for brookies, but standard insect imitations and egg patterns also work on all but the biggest fish. Brookies are fall spawners.

Golden Trout

Golden trout were originally found in the High Sierras of California and now live in many waters of the Rockies. There is a mystique about goldens because they cruise only the high-elevation lakes and streams in wilderness areas. When introduced to lower-elevation waters, they lose their brilliant colors and look just like rainbows, with which they then interbreed.

Only in waters over 8,000 feet in elevation do they retain the brilliance that has made them a rare prize sought after by an adventurous few.

Goldens exist mainly in high-country areas where a stream runs between two or more natural lakes; other waters must be stocked regularly. They are mainly insectivorous but also feed heavily on scuds and leeches. Stream goldens will hit dry flies well, but lake goldens seldom rise to the surface, preferring nymphs and scuds. The largest goldens are lake dwellers; stream fish are usually small. Big goldens in streams are almost always lake fish on spawning runs, which occur in the spring — June or July in the high country.

I consider goldens to have the longest memory of any trout. The big, lake goldens are notoriously difficult to catch, despite a short fishing season and their remote location. High-elevation fish can grow slowly and live longer than their lowland cousins; a 20-inch fish might be over 10 years old. These fish will cruise the lake perimeter but tend to congregate in inlet and outlet areas and in the adjacent bays.

Char

Char are a trout-like family that includes brookies, Arctic char, Dolly Varden, bull trout, and lake trout (mackinaw). Dolly Varden and Arctic char are common in Alaska, Canada, Siberia, and adjacent areas and are difficult to tell apart. They are mostly meat eaters, feeding only on insects when they are young fish. Bull trout are similar but inhabit inland waterways like those in Montana and eastern Oregon.

Lake trout are seldom seen in rivers except on their fall spawning runs, and they can spawn in lakes as well. They were originally found in the glacial-shield lakes and have been transplanted to many of the bigger, deeper western reservoirs, flourishing wherever there is a supply of chubs, suckers, trout, or kokanee. Northern fish have slow growth rates but grow large because they live a long time, sometimes more than a hundred years. They feed on nymphs and scuds only at a young age but will key in on crayfish if baitfish are scarce. Fly fishing for lake trout is possible only in northern lakes and streams (where the water is shallow enough for fly tackle) or in September (when the fish come into the shallows at night to spawn).

Of all the char, only brookies regularly feed on nymphs, but they will all feed on eggs and nymph-fished minnow imitations when they are found in shallow water.

Grayling and Whitefish

Montana grayling are endangered and difficult to find in their original drainages. They still live in a few lakes and even fewer streams. Their northern cousin, the Arctic grayling, is much more common in waters of northern Canada and Alaska. Europe also has a variety of grayling.

Grayling are mainly insect feeders and are regularly fished with dry flies, nymphs, eggs, or wet flies. Only the largest grayling feed on minnows, because their small mouth is designed for small foods. Nymphing with #14 to #18 flies is quite effective.

Whitefish are common in some trout streams. They are considered trash fish by some and good sport fish by others. A nympher generally likes whitefish because if they are being caught, the angler knows he is nymphing where trout are lurking. Whitefish will also fill in the action on days when trout fishing is slow. If you are catching too many whitefish, move into the faster water upstream or concentrate on a perfectly natural drift. Whitefish often prefer a little drag on the nymphs, while selective trout prefer an entirely natural drift.

You can actually switch to catching a different species of fish in a single body of water just by changing your presentation and offering your patterns in other spots.

In *Fly Fishing for Trout: Volume Three — Small Fly Techniques,* a companion volume in the Library, I went into some detail on trout habits in relation to small flies. The following section will brush on these habits and relate how trout see nymphs and how they use various water types and structures.

How Trout Learn

Although much of trout's daily routine is instinctual, they do have the ability to learn. Learning is accomplished by a combination of survival instinct and conditioned response. If people are common on trout streams, trout need to learn how to deal with their presence. On some streams, if trout quit feeding and hid every time an angler waded near, they might starve to death. Trout are survivors and actually adapt to accept humans as a natural part of their environment. They are more selective when anglers are around, but they won't stop feeding. Each encounter with anglers adds to their conditioning. After an uneducated trout is caught easily on a dry fly and then released, it recognizes that a food source is not safe. Natural wariness kicks in and it becomes more conscious of unnatural aspects to its foods.

The most common turnoff for trout is an angler's unnatural presentation. They may see dozens of bad presentations in a single day. Some trout reject unnaturally drifting items and others notice insect size or surface impression. If the leader tied on your fly is too obvious, or if the fly has unnatural drag, the educated fish will reject it.

Selectivity

Trout have small brains and are unable to analyze everything. They do, however, have the ability to focus on one or two aspects of their foods and act very quickly on that information. Each experience adds to their conditioning. Each selective fish may develop slightly different things it keys in on; this is the reason educated trout continually frustrate anglers. Trout condition themselves against the things anglers throw at them most regularly, and each fish may be different. Once conditioned, the fish will reject frequently seen fly patterns and presentation errors (including sloppy casts and unnatural drift), improper fly size, improper shape or surface impression, and so on.

Foods that are commonly fed on become imprinted on a trout's brain. If a particular food fits this basic imprint, the trout will accept it. But anything that falls outside the parameters of that imprint will be ignored. This reaction could be likened to a potato-chip inspector at a potato-chip factory. Before long, anything unnatural in the chips is instantly recognized and rejected, with little thought.

Exact Imitation

When trout get ultra-selective to naturals, exact imitation and presentation become important. Anglers proficient at exact imitation and presentation become highly effective. Because nymphing trout are often less wary than trout feeding on the surface, a good nympher can get an extraordinarily large portion of the fishing action even where trout are quite selective.

Most fly rodders use dry flies. Because these are easy for trout to see errors in, they quickly become suspect. Nymphs are the trout's next best choice. Nymphers tend to offer improper nymph sizes and present them poorly, so nymphing trout can often feed heavily with little danger of being caught. If nymphing is common, trout key in on smaller nymphs, which are abundant and even harder to fish properly. Fish exact patterns carefully and systematically, especially to trout you are actually able to see.

Attractor Flies

Trout also learn through natural curiosity, sampling their environment, which is why they adapt to so many different waters. Trout will sample just about anything in their world that is not perceived as a threat. This is where attractor flies come in. But remember that if attractors are commonly used, trout get used to them easily, too. The idea is to show them something different. If trout are selective to average-sized artificials, your attractor nymphs should be small or extra large. If everyone uses brown #14 Pheasant Tail Nymphs, try a #18 in olive, orange, or chartreuse. Small sizes are in keeping with the size imprint, and larger attractors trigger opportunistic feeding action. That's why hot local patterns change almost every year. And fly tyers have the advantage because they can tie many custom flies easily.

Attractor flies also have built-in triggers. White wings and rubber legs often trigger a feeding response, as do brown, black, peacock herl, and flash components. The rest of the fly may not matter to the trout at all. Once you figure out what type of trigger works best, you should have a good day of fishing. Cover lots of water with attractor-nymph patterns to get the most opportunistic fish. Typical attractor nymphs include the Prince Nymph and the Girdle Bug, and they are fished either natural-drift or on the move.

Suggestive Patterns

The other main fly type is the suggestive pattern, such as the Fur Bug, Gold-Ribbed Hare's Ear, or Woolly Bugger. These flies are designed to imitate nothing in particular and many things in general. Because you leave the interpretation of the food item to the trout, you can simulate many foods at once. Suggestive nymphs are usually low-tech, nondescript lumps. They are not used by many anglers who opt for exact or attractor nymphs, but they are very effective. They work especially well in waters you are not familiar with, fished to search the area for feeders.

A Fur Bug can simulate a scud, sow bug, leech, mayfly nymph, caddis larva, caddis pupa, terrestrial, small minnow, small crayfish, or egg. The fly matches the imprint for food on the fish's mind, and the lack of detail lets the trout interpret the pattern as whatever it wants the imitation to be. Suggestives are usually fished natural-drift or slow retrieve.

Trout Structure

Trout do not relate to structure quite as much as largemouth bass do, but they relate to foods and cover that become recognizable. Reading the water is very important for finding nymphing trout. Just noticing the type of water will often tell you what type of nymphing is required to catch the trout there.

In lakes, trout use what are called *feeding lanes,* sort of trout highways with lots of roadside eateries. Trout will cruise back and forth along weedbeds, drop-offs, old river channels, channels in weedbeds, and scum lines (or wind-drift lines). They may feed in open water occasionally (baitfish feeders in big lakes especially, or daphnia feeders) but usually relate to structure that is unseen. A fishfinder or sidefinder is more valuable for finding structure than for finding fish. Once you know which type of structure the trout are relating to, you can narrow down your search considerably.

Weedlines in shallow areas of lakes are particularly productive, providing much cover for insects and crustaceans. The trout will cruise until a food item can easily be intercepted between weeds.

Rocky points and the bowls between points of bays are great areas as well. Trout change depths as the day or season progresses but will generally be somewhere close by. They cruise the perimeter of lakes looking for food. Areas of food concentration are also areas of trout concentration.

If the water is clear, leaders should be longer and lighter than those used in murky water, which is a type of structure as well. You can approach fish more closely in murky water. Crystal-clear waters might require small, exact patterns, while murky waters are best fished with bulky flies that fish can find more easily. The old saying "Dark day, dark fly; bright day, bright fly" is a place to start.

In rivers, reading the water is easier. Many of the water types are easy to identify. Anglers tend to ignore rapids, assuming that because of the speed of the current, trout couldn't be there. But remember that rapids are caused by big rocks, and big rocks create good holding water. Some of the biggest trout in any given piece of water can be caught on nymphs in fast water. Big trout handle fast water better than small trout, and the cover and food available in rapids create prime lies. The biggest, most aggressive fish generally take the best lies. If you can get your fly down to the trout through the fast water, you have a good chance at finding the bigger trout.

Look for pockets behind boulders, and deep channels and drop-offs. Weighted flies and leaders are a must, and you should match fly size to water type. Rapids usually have stoneflies or larger caddis larvae, aquatic redworms, or craneflies. Flies sizes 10 to 2 are usual, unless the fish are very selective, in which case you should go smaller, but seldom below #16. Fish must be able to see the fly in the fast water. Exact patterns are seldom necessary; visibility of the fly and presentation level are more important.

The deep, swift runs below rapids are also big trout areas. These channels often produce many fine fish, which move up or down to them when nymphs are drifting en masse. Here again, fly level is important. The fly must get down fast and drift just off the bottom. Big flies are the rule, but trout will also take small flies. These channels are great places for trout to intercept nearly any kind of food. Nymphing streamers here often nets some big trout. Work these areas thoroughly, with several nymph patterns.

Where the current cuts into a bank and creates a deep, swift bend, you can be sure the trout are lurking. Food is concentrated in the bend, and the undercut bank or deeper water provides protection. Stumps, old car bodies, and boulders in these areas often hold big fish. If you aren't losing occasional flies on snags, you are not fishing these areas properly.

Riffles are the broken surfaces of fairly shallow areas of fast water. They are the food factories of many trout streams. Because food is plentiful and the broken surface gives them a sense of security, trout often line up in riffles and feed heavily on nymphs and scuds. You can almost always be sure that a fish in a riffle is feeding. The exception to this rule is that rainbows and cutthroat trout spawn in riffles. Browns usually prefer tailouts or current seams along shore.

Riffle trout will hold in fast water and intercept food. Any depression in the gravel or rocks blocking the current will hold fish. The gravel bars that drop off into deeper water are hot spots because fish can feed shallow there and retreat to deep water quickly.

Nymphing in riffles is fairly easy, and the riffles are full of mayfly, caddis, midge, and some stonefly nymphs, as well as scuds, sow bugs, aquatic worms, and drowned terrestrials. Don't overlook any part of the riffle; the trout can be in water as shallow as six inches deep. Shallow-water nymphing is quite enthralling. Wading knee-deep before you begin fishing will spook many trout, so you should start casting back from the bank and work right in close. Riffles may be almost empty of trout until nymphing action heats up, when fish move up from the deeper water just below. The trout follow the best nymphing action and so should you. Fish the deeper water below riffles with nymph patterns until the action speeds up, then gradually move into faster water.

Pools have traditionally been poor areas for nymphing. There are almost always trout in pools, but they are resting more often than feeding. In wintertime, however, trout get lethargic from the cold water, and since they cannot fight swift currents, they drop back into deeper water to conserve energy. Contrary to popular opinion, trout do feed all winter. They won't move far, though, and you must almost bump them in the nose with your nymph before you get their attention.

I was fishing the Provo River near my home one winter when it started snowing. The water was so cold that the snow collected in the eddies, rather than melting. My thermometer showed the water was down to just 32.5 degrees F. Surprisingly, trout and whitefish were still active. They sat in the small pools below fast water and took nymphs that were bounced right into their mouths. A fly several inches too high didn't work. Don't assume that because the water is cold, the trout are also inactive. Just go where the fish go in cold water, and present the fly carefully.

Nymphing a pool requires a high level of concentration. Strikes are very delicate. The best areas in a pool are where the current concentrates foam bubbles and other river scum. Trout will hold on the bottom, under the floating debris at the surface, and collect the sunken edibles. These current seams may hold 90 percent of the feeding fish in the pool though they make up only 10 percent of the area.

Rapids or falls that dump into slow pools are hot spots. The biggest fish are often right in the plunge pool, picking off edibles that are forced down to the bottom by the current. Smaller fish generally hold toward the tails of plunge pools.

Eddies are the back currents normally found in bays and slow-water areas off the main current. They spin in a slow vortex, catching food items. Trout are usually selective feeders here, often staying suspended off the bottom, under the foam or scum lines on the current seams.

Flats are the wide, flat, slick-surfaced areas of slow to moderate currents. Skill and delicacy are required to nymph these areas, where anglers use greased-leader and other light nymphing rigs. Trout generally feed on small nymphs and scuds here. When spooked, the fish will shoot up or down into deeper water and won't return for a while. They are exposed to predators but will feed there anyway, especially when midges are hatching or when light levels are low in the evening and the nymph drift is an easy target.

Some streams such as typical spring creeks can be called flats and are usually carpeted with a rich weedbed. Because weedbeds are difficult to nymph, concentrate on the channels between weedbeds and the drop-offs into deeper water. Trout will often hide under weedbeds and pick off nymphs drifting by in the channels. I've spent many pleasant hours in a tree or on a bridge above a weedy flat, watching trout feed and looking for that giant tail waving underneath a weedbank. Any clean gravel spots in the weeds are also prime targets for nymphers. Regularly inspect your nymph to see if it is trailing weeds, for trout seldom take weedy flies.

A tailout is the section of stream or river where the water from the flats or pools picks up speed at the top of rapids or riffles. The surface of the water is flat, but current speeds and a narrowing stream flow condense the foods drifting down, attracting trout. Just a slight depression in the gravel or weedbeds is enough to hold trout.

Once you find productive types of water to nymph, make mental or paper notes. Those areas change seasonally, but the action will be the same at the same time next year. You might plan on a general feeding-lie rotation for nymphing. In spring, trout line up on current edges, drop-offs, or spawning areas, usually just above their deeper wintering lies. Fish the runs and tops of pools. In summer, trout often move into riffles and rapids and retreat into pools to rest or feed on scum lines.

Nymph the faster water for best results. In fall, midge hatches and spawning activity move many browns into the tailouts. Rainbows will still be found in the faster runs. And in winter, trout find feeding lies in the slow, deeper water adjacent to currents. Fish the deep runs below spawning waters. Concentrate on the slower runs and pools.

NYMPHING LEVELS

Strike-zone accuracy and fly-drift level are what separate the pros from the wannabes. There is no secret fly pattern that will work if your presentation does not get the fly where the trout will take it. Remember that presentation accounts for 75 percent of your success rate.

Fly Presentation Levels

Divide a lake or stream into three equal levels. The upper level is where trout feed on dry flies, terrestrials, and emerging (hatching) insects. Trout either suspend under the surface or else rise from the bottom to feed here. Nymphing opportunities are plenty just before and during hatches. Non-hatch periods allow for little if any upper-level nymphing.

The middle level in streams is where most fishermen put their nymphs, but trout don't use this section very often. Trout follow their food. If it's on the surface, they go there; if it's along the bottom, they stay down. Only during the short period when insects are traveling up to the surface are they available in the middle.

The middle level in lakes is somewhat different from the middle level in streams because there is no current and a cruising trout can simply adjust its trajectory to intercept a food in the middle level. Still, it makes more sense to present the fly at the level where the trout spend the most time feeding.

Fly Presentation Levels

The lower level is of prime consideration to the angler. Ninety percent of a trout's food is subsurface, and 90 percent of that subsurface food is taken in the lower third (depthwise). This lower level is where good nymphers concentrate their presentations much of the time, year-round.

Trout are not designed to grub the bottom like whitefish or carp. Rather, they feed at nose level or up, seldom down. Although trout are often observed tail up, rooting in the weedbeds, they are almost always just shaking bugs loose. Actual feeding is done at normal levels after the insects are dislodged. Normal nymphing levels are from one to 12 inches off the bottom — nose level and up. Most nymphers don't get their flies into this zone very often, and only the most aggressive trout will rise to take patterns from the middle water. Good nymphers have a high degree of concentration when nymphing, to assure the nymphs are down in the major strike zone.

Strike Zones

Remember those days when it seemed the trout just weren't biting? Things were slow, and any action was inconsistent and scarce, or nonexistent. Those are the days nymphers have an advantage over all other fly fishermen. Little can be done to change the trout's attitude on a particularly slow day, but a lot can be done, in the form of presentation techniques, to increase your success rate. The next chapter deals with these nymphing techniques, which work in almost any condition any time of year. Here I will discuss what happens to the trout on slow fishing days.

The best fishing days are when trout are aggressive, hit almost anything, and move a long distance to take the fly. The distance they move is known as the *strike zone.* Large strike zones can be from 10 to 25 feet in diameter. Enjoy these; they don't happen often. Above-average aggressive fish will move two to 10 feet to take a morsel of food, but on the average, trout will move four inches to two feet to take flies. If trout are selective — due to high fishing pressure, much practice of catch-and-release, changing weather patterns, dropping water temperatures, rising water levels, darkening water color, or something less noticeable, like how full the fish feels — the trout will have smaller and smaller strike zones. It's not uncommon for trout to move only 1/2 inch to four inches to eat. That's a maximum of four inches up or to either side, a one to eight-inch diameter of opportunity.

If your nymph does not get into that zone, forget catching that trout. Now imagine the fish in two to six feet of water. How often can haphazard casting get the fly into that small strike zone? Not often. Typically, a nympher's fly will just be getting down to the right level when drag occurs and the fly swings up at the end of the drift. The proper nymphing technique in this situation requires you to do everything possible to keep the fly down near the bottom and drifting at a level so the fish can just open its mouth and take the fly without moving a fin. When trout are in an energy-conservation mode — in selective or low-feeding periods — this is the only technique that consistently works. I'll talk more about this later.

VISUAL VERSUS MENTAL ACUITY

Trout have a marvelous set of instincts and senses that allows them to interact with their environment. You now know that trout are not intelligent, forward-thinking creatures with voluminous memories, but at the instinctual and reactionary level, they are quite advanced. A trout's reactions are about 20 times faster than our own. If something does not taste right, it is spat out quickly. If a trout is spooked, it splits at high speed in just a fraction of a second. Trout have two things on their simple minds — safety and food.

Presenting your fly and yourself to the trout naturally is the best bet for success. We know that trout get a mental picture of foods imprinted on their brain and additional information is ignored. That is why selective trout do not react to the big hook sticking out of the nymph's belly.

A nympher will discover that the good triggers in a streamer are unnatural swimming motions (that is, motions that make the fly look like an injured or frightened minnow), the general shape of the fly, and the streamer's eye. Predators may key in on a baitfish eye, which therefore becomes both the trigger and the target. Nymph triggers are natural presentation and fly shape, texture, and color. I believe that trout do see color but it ranks quite low on the list of priorities for matching natural foods, with a few exceptions, such as scuds, eggs, or nymphs fished in very clear, slow water. But even there, presentation is more important than color. Don't ignore color, however, because it does make a difference.

Attractors have other triggers besides "hunger + food = feeding." Curiosity, aggression, and dominance are all factors. They sort of appeal to the emotional side of trout rather than the intellectual.

A trout cannot see clearly at distances but it can see the shapes and motions out of water quite well. A bird flying overhead triggers a speedy retreat because a bird may be a predator. Humans also trigger flight in an uneducated trout. Educated trout in catch-and-release waters break natural programming to accept humans as part of their environment. Some trout become so bold that they use the current break made by wading anglers to rest and feed behind. Trout can learn to seek out wading anglers for the food they kick up. This is a learned response to unnatural stimuli.

In most waters, however, human presence is considered suspect, and when it is detected, trout will quit feeding, go for cover, or get much more selective. Once you spook a trout, you have little chance of catching that fish. Selective feeding can be dealt with, but more important, if you never make your presence known in the first place, the trout becomes much more vulnerable. The fish does not stop feeding, nor does it hide or become extra-selective. Wear bland, earthy, unflashy colors that blend with streamside vegetation or the sky. Move slowly and keep a low profile. If possible, use cover and fish from behind a big rock or brush. I often stand beneath an overhanging limb in the shade to fish tree-lined runs. Stomping right into the trout's cone of vision is not the recommended method for catching that fish.

Presenting yourself as non-threatening is a major advantage. That is why we have all heard that we should sneak up on trout, sometimes called "skulking for trout." Incautious wading produces low and high-frequency vibrations that trout sense with their lateral line. Dirt banks also transfer vibrations through the ground as you walk.

The lateral line is part of the trout's highly evolved sense of touch. Next time you catch a trout or other gamefish, look for the faint, narrow line that extends the length of the body, on each flank. This is evidence of an intricate nervous system capable of feeling what's happening around the fish. Any more sensitive and it would be as good as a bat's radar or a dolphin's sonar.

The fewer sound clues you give to the fish, the better your chances. Just as you are comfortable walking alone through a forest until you suddenly hear a twig snap behind you, so is a trout carefree until a clue tells it to be cautious. Wade slowly and quietly. Voices above water don't transmit underwater well, but a rock grinding against another as you step on it does, like fingernails scraping on a blackboard. Just trudging through the water creates sounds of water displacement that are unnatural to the trout. If you are the first one to fish a run and you do so quietly, you are likely to have good results. If it has already been fished by several people, expect very selective fish. In short, become a stealth or Rambo nympher for best success.

In regard to fly choice, a trout sees more than feels a nymph. Streamers make low-frequency vibrations that trout feel, but few nymphs are designed to be felt. In fast water, shape and size are the most important clues to trout. The trout sees a blur of food-like movement and has only a second to decide whether or not to eat it. Exact imitation in this situation is unnecessary. In slow water, trout have time to come up close to the fly and examine it. More exact imitations through size, shape, and color are in order. The closer the trout is, the clearer its view of the fly.

Rejections of the pattern mean that something is wrong. In fast water, hooking no fish usually indicates an improper fly-drift level or the improper simulation of food items. In slow water, natural, drag-free presentation becomes more and more critical. Besides the look of the fly, any aberration in natural drift is noticed by the trout because it is up close and has time to look at the pattern. A fly dragging in the current is unnatural, and only aggressive, uneducated trout will fall for the bad presentation. In stillwater, presentation level is very important, as is fly speed.

OVERLEAF: *Fall nymphing on the Bighorn.*

CHAPTER THREE

TECHNIQUES AND RIGGING

Regardless of how effective a particular fly, how carefully chosen your fishing spot, and how expensive your fishing equipment, you are not likely to catch very many fish if your presentation technique is poor. I've always believed that if you understand the reasons you are supposed to do something, you will do a much better job. The information in the earlier chapters on trout foods, habits, species, and holding-water types was all given to prepare a mental picture of the stream, lake, and trout so that the following section on presentation techniques might make the most sense.

NYMPHING DYNAMICS

Nymphing dynamics are the aspects of presentation that every nympher should understand but few do. These dynamics include things like the sink rate of the fly, primary and secondary targets, keeping the pattern in the strike zone, and slack control. Experienced nymphers have found that the cast-and-let-drift technique is seldom effective on selective trout. Completely drag-free drift is impossible, but you need to get as close to it as you can. Some trout prefer movement by the fly, while most prefer a natural, drag-free drift.

Fly Sink Rate

Each fly sinks at a different rate. Big, heavily weighted flies sink quickly, while small, unweighted flies sink slowly. The leader diameter also affects sink rates, with a heavy leader sinking the slowest. All flies have weight, but the materials added, and even the hook size and wire gauge, can change sink rates. One reason so many people like bead-head nymphs is because they work. The extra weight helps get the fly down into the strike zone better, and the weight helps level the fly out, displaying the fly at a different angle than usual. The flash may help, too, but fly-drift level is particularly improved, which improves hookups.

The sink rate can determine where your fly is fished. Small, unweighted nymphs are good for fishing in the upper third or in shallow riffles. Heavy nymphs are best in deep, fast water.

A big debate has been going on for years about whether flies should be weighted, or just the leader, or if weight should be used at all. I like to use weighted flies in fast water and unweighted flies in slow or shallow water. Weighted flies have less natural movement but are necessary for getting down behind rocks quickly or into channels in fast water. Weighted leaders get you down reasonably fast, but the fly trails up higher until it has a chance to sink to the correct level.

In lakes and areas where retrieved nymphs are used, I weight the head of the fly lightly (with bead-heads or lead wraps) so that the fly sinks level or jigs slightly. Unweighted flies still have a heavy hook bend that makes the fly ride almost vertically until being retrieved. Sinking fly lines help get the fly to the right depth in lakes and some streams.

My river system uses no extra weight in #16 nymphs and smaller. Nymphs sizes 14 to 10 have some weight (lead under the body, heavy wire ribbing, or bead-head), and #8 to #1 nymphs are fairly well weighted. In these cases, the fly size generally corresponds with the water type: small flies, slow or shallow water; medium flies, moderately fast or deep current; big nymphs, fast, deep water. Extra weight can always be added to the leader as circumstances require. I'll go into this in depth in the section entitled "Weight Options."

Primary and Secondary Targets

When casting your nymphing rig, you need to be aware of sink rates, but you should also be aware of how far above your primary target you need to cast in order to let the flies sink into the strike zone. The primary target is always the fish or the fish holding water. The secondary target is where the fly actually lands on the water surface, upstream of the primary target. In fast, deep water, most people have a problem with this because the fly is seldom cast far enough upstream to allow enough time for sinking. Some anglers try to compensate by adding too much weight, which does get the fly down but is a pain to cast and snags up too often, creating frustration.

Ideally, nymphers should cast far enough upstream so that the weighted or unweighted fly has plenty of room to sink before reaching the strike zone, where it should then be kept as long as reasonably possible. Sight-nymphing to shallow fish is exciting, but when fish are not visible, just concentrate on fishing the trout holding water. If one cast does not get down fast enough, cast farther upstream next time, or wade upstream, or add some weight.

In lakes, trout are generally cruising, so the fly must be cast far enough in front of the fish to avoid spooking it and also to give the fly time to sink to the right depth before the retrieve is begun. Calculating the vector of the moving fish and the sinking fly is sometimes tricky when sight-casting to individual fish but it is not a problem otherwise. In the shallows, you can let the nymph rest on the bottom well ahead of the fish's projected course, and when the fish gets close, you can then move the fly to attract the fish's attention. When trout or cruising lanes are not visible, the countdown method should be used. Let the fly sink to various counts before beginning retrieves; five-count — retrieve, or 10-count — retrieve, or 15-count — retrieve. When the trout's feeding level is found, return to that count on the next cast.

Slack Control

Nothing is more important to nymphing success than line control. Two anglers can have identical tackle and flies, but the angler who handles the fly line properly can catch two or three times more than the other. I guided trout fly fishers for nine years in Alaska, Idaho, Montana, and Utah, and found that only about five percent of the anglers could control slack and nymph-drift properly. Once the rest caught on and got in the groove, their success rates went way up.

Line manipulation is part casting and part mending. I will assume you have studied casting and know that a mend is a correction in the fly line, done with the rod, to reduce unnatural drag on the floating fly line (in other words, to get rid of fly-line belly).

Here is why line control is so important. The typical nymphing cast is up-and-across stream. The fly begins to sink, but the current catching and bellying the line causes some drag. Once the least bit of tension occurs on the line, the fly sinks more slowly and may never get down into the strike zone before swinging up at the end of the drift.

To try to combat this, most nymphers make an upstream mend somewhere during the drift and get a longer drift. One mend is okay, but it causes a big "S"-curve in the line. This reduces the drag, but there is still a fair amount of drag unless currents are perfect, which they seldom are.

You might not notice much drag yourself, but the trout is up close and is able to see even small unnatural movements. Think about sitting down at a fast-food restaurant. You open your hamburger wrapping and before you grab the burger it starts slinking away under its own power. Would it make you suspicious? Unnatural drag alerts the trout, especially a selective, educated trout, that something is wrong — just enough to cause it to reject the fly. As I said earlier, perfectly natural drift is next to impossible, but it should be every stream nympher's goal. That means slack control, which means lots of on-water slack in your line so the current can act on it without dragging the fly.

Few people put enough slack line on the water, fearing that they won't be able to set the hook with lots of slack. Our casting instructors show us how to make beautiful, straight casts, and to some, an ugly, wiggly cast is an abomination. But if you never get the hits in the first place, why worry about setting the hook or making pretty casts? Besides, when you learn to reach-cast, make the line land with slack on the water, mend at the right moment, manipulate lots of little "S"-curves into your line, and watch and imagine your nymphs drifting a long way through the strike zone, you are getting a beautifully natural drift. Then you know you're in the groove, and you can almost anticipate the fish hitting. It is the difference between someone stomping across a stage and a beautiful ballet. A straight line is not always the best thing.

Each nymphing technique that is described later in this chapter has a unique way of controlling slack. Slack control is extremely important in nymphing.

NYMPHING GEAR

Gear does not make a fly fisherman, but proper gear can help him just as much as the proper tool can help an auto mechanic. You can find fly rods from $10 to $2000, reels from $15 to $1000 and fly lines from $5 to more than $50. A high-cost outfit does not mean you will fish that much better. I fished with a $17 graphite fly rod every week for a couple years, and I got quite good at nymphing with it. Expensive rods and reels give you high-quality construction, expensive components, and extensive selection. Cheaper rods and reels use common materials and cheaper components and offer fewer selections, but they still work.

I worked in several retail fly shops over the years, and people were always asking which fly rod was the best. I'd grab the most expensive one off the rack, watch them gasp at the price, and then recommend they get the best they can afford, putting the most into the rod, the second into a good line, and the least into the reel.

For most trout-fishing purposes, the reel simply holds the line. When you can afford a better reel, just upgrade and use the first as a backup reel. But when you fish water where fish over 20 inches can take out substantial amounts of line, your reel should have enough drag to keep the spool from over-running when line is stripped off quickly. This may mean a more expensive reel.

I suggest a reel that will hold at least 50 yards of backing. You'll seldom use the backing, but when you need it, you'll be glad it's there. It also helps fill a spool. The larger diameter the reel, the more line can be reeled up with each turn of the handle. Small-diameter spools take a long time to reel up slack line, and they kink up the line more. I prefer narrow, large-diameter reels.

In streams, 90 percent of my nymphing is done with a floating line. In lakes, 90 percent is done with sinking fly lines. Several major manufacturers carry a huge array of fly-line weights, densities, tapers, and finishes. Fly lines priced from $5 to $20 are either level (no taper) or inexpensive tapered lines. State-of-the-art fly lines are $30 to more than $50. Cheaper lines generally don't last as long, don't have slick finishes, and are offered in smaller selections. Expensive lines give you the best floating and best shooting finishes and lots of tapers and densities to choose from.*

For trout nymphing, I have found the long-belly, weight-forward lines the most useful floating lines for streams. Two others of value are a Type I or II sinking line, for typical stillwater nymphing, and a fast-sink, sink-tip line, for certain fast-water and big-fly techniques.

Keep your lines cleaned and conditioned for best performance. A dirty floating line won't float or shoot well and makes mending a chore.

Nymphing rods are usually eight to 10 feet long. Their length helps in mending the line, picking up deep or weighted nymphs out of the water, and setting the hook. A stiff butt and a medium to fast-action tip are recommended. Slow-action rods are preferred by some anglers, but I find these rods sluggish for setting the hook and not very powerful in windy conditions. Short, five to seven-foot-long light rods work well on small, brushy streams where a long rod can't cast.

Most fly shops recommend rods in the 6 to 8-weight range for nymphing. Those rods are fine for fast water and for big, weighted flies with heavier tippets. Much of the nymphing I do, however, is with a much lighter rod. I generally use a nine-foot, stiff-action, 3 to 5-weight rod. Light lines are much better for typical stream-nymphing situations because their fine diameter and limp nature allow the currents to bend and twist them easily. They also drag less when submerged. Heavier lines are stiffer, which can cause unwanted drag, and they splash down harder, which can spook wary trout. Since much of my nymphing is done with light tippets and for selective fish, light lines and the rods they match offer me the best combination

---

Also see chapter 4 of *Presenting the Fly* by Lefty Kreh—Ed.

for fishing up to #6 nymphs, weighted. You'll find that once you learn how to cast weighted flies, you can cast surprisingly heavy rigs on light rods.

In rapids and deep runs and on big, windy rivers, I go to a 9 or 9 1/2-footer balanced for a 6 or 7-weight line. Big, weighted nymphs can be cast long, even in windy conditions, and are easier to cast with this heavier setup. The fast water masks the line slap and extra drag produced by the heavier line. Rods 10 feet or longer make great mending levers and cast long, but I find them a bit unwieldy for anything but big, brawling rivers and big flies, when I'm feeling macho. If you want only one rod for all trouting needs, I would suggest a western (stiff) action nine-footer for a 5-weight line. If you fish mainly fast water or for large fish, make that a 6-weight.

STRIKE INDICATORS

Strike indicators, or SIs, are some of the most valuable tools a nympher can have. Before SIs became popular, nymphing was a sport reserved for a dedicated few who could walk on water and leap tall trees in a single bound — or at least appeared to have some sixth sense. Actually, nymphers were just responding to subtle visual clues, such as the flash of a subsurface feeding fish, the twitch of the leader or line tip, or the feel of the take on a slightly taut line.

I had tried nymphing several times by the early 70s, and my only hookups were by accident. You know: I'd pick up the line to cast and a fish would be there. So I mainly stuck with dry flies. My fly-fishing club put on a mini-conclave around 1977 with Dave Whitlock as the star. He introduced me to the orange fly-line-coating strike indicators he used, which were threaded onto his leader. This was before strike indicators were available commercially. I was intrigued and tried them out. They worked well, and my nymphing skills and my catch went up tenfold.

Few people were nymphing with SIs when I started guiding the Henry's Fork in Idaho in 1983. Some anglers even scoffed at my nymphing techniques, until I proved they could double or triple their catch rates. Regardless of your skill level, SIs will improve your success. They have been shown to be a valid tool, not just another gimmick.

SIs are basically bobbers for fly outfits. If you think about it, a floating leader and your fly line itself are also SIs because they help indicate strikes. Adding a more visible strike indicator will improve hookups, improve system adjustability, and improve natural-drift capability.

Typical SI materials include foam, cork, fly-line coating, synthetic or wool tow yarn, balsa, CDC clumps, and dry flies. Orvis has even come out with a marshmallow-like, moldable, biodegradable indicator material. All these materials float and should be chosen to match conditions. Most anglers use one SI, but several styles in several colors will cover more water types and trout habits. Common colors are pink, red, orange, chartreuse, and white. The brightest colors help you see the indicator even in glare or low-light situations. Some sunglass colors almost cancel out certain SI colors, so find a color that you can see at distances when you're wearing your polarized sunglasses.

Brightly colored SIs may distract selective trout, however, and smaller white or light pink indicators, or dry-fly indicators, may be better for conditioned, educated trout. Just as trout can reject commonly seen fly patterns and be turned off by drift flaws, they can learn to stop feeding or swerve away momentarily as a gaudy SI floats overhead. If you think trout are avoiding your SI, go to a less obtrusive model.

Strike indicators attach to the leader in many different ways. Foam or cork SIs require toothpicks, yarn SIs use knots, self-adhesive SIs just pinch on, and dry flies can be tied to the leader as SIs, with a dropper tippet tied to the nymph below.

Pick an indicator that matches the water. In fast water when heavy flies are used, you will likely need a large, buoyant, highly visible model. SIs that have sunk underwater are almost useless and will distract the trout even more. In slow water when small, unweighted flies are being cast, use a small SI, the smallest you can keep in sight. Experiment with SI types until you find the ones that suit you, your techniques, and the waters you fish.

The most common problems with SIs are, again, line control and slack control. The strike indicator should always be positioned directly above or downstream from the fly. If the fly lands on fast water and the indicator on slow water, the fly will soon be downstream from the indicator and the SI will not be of much help. Try to keep the fly and the indicator at the same current speeds.

The line should be mended so that it is positioned generally above the SI, with plenty of slack. A belly below the SI will cause drag and considerably reduce takes on standard nymphing rigs. Each mend should be made as close as you can to the SI while you move the fly as little as possible. Use a half roll cast, half mend to do this. As soon as the mend is made, more slack should be wiggled out the rod tip to reintroduce the slack that the mend eliminated. Most people strip in line after a mend rather than letting more slack out, a common mistake that reduces natural drift considerably.

Your strike indicator tells you many things, so be sure to watch it very closely. If it's going faster than the current or the bubbles next to it, your drift is improper and you must mend or introduce more slack. If it is drifting at the same speed as the bubbles around it, it is drifting with the current. If it is moving slightly slower than the current, your flies are down in the strike zone, and you can expect a hit.

If the SI is twitching rhythmically, the split-shot is probably bouncing on the bottom. If the indicator hesitates, set the hook. It may be a rock, a weed, or a fish. Never assume it is just the bottom or you may well miss a hit. If your rig is set up properly, the SI should seldom drag the bottom but ride just above it.

I try to imagine the nymphs riding on a thin pillow of water just above the rocks. Then the slightest hesitation or unnatural movement can be considered a take and the hook can be set. Developing a fast reaction time for hooksets is important with most nymphing techniques. Learn to read the SI and interpret what it's telling you about your drift, about strikes, and about the current.

Too often you can be half-watching the SI but not really focusing on it. Concentrate on every aspect of the SI, and use your peripheral vision to see the line and how it's drifting or perhaps see a trout's flash as it takes the fly. Physical contact with the SI (that is, a slightly taut line) seems natural to many fly fishers but only works in faster water, up close on short casts. Most of the time, a taut line means the flies are dragging unnaturally. More often than not, your contact should be all visual and mental.

WEIGHT OPTIONS

Weight is an important component of most nymphing rigs. There are many options available to anglers today, including split-shot of various sizes and styles, from cannonballs to micro split-shot and removable split-shot. Other choices are the new non-lead weighting systems, which are soon to be the standard, if not the law; lead putty; fluorocarbon leader sections; weighted flies, including bead-heads; lead-core sinkers; and, of course, sinking lines.

Lead is still the most often used, cheapest, and most versatile way to get your flies down into the strike zone. Every nympher should have one micro split-shot and some size B and BB removable split-shot, the kind with little wings on the back for easy removal.

Micro split-shot is used with all but the shallowest nymphing rigs. It is placed four to 10 inches from the fly so that the fly can still move naturally but stays down. Trout in a few waters will spit out the fly if they feel the weight hit their side, so a greater distance between the fly and the micro split-shot may be required.

Larger split-shot will help you get the flies down fast but is difficult to cast. Good presentation techniques make it possible for you to use half the weight that someone with constant drag on his line needs to get down to the same level. A heavy weight is necessary, however, for getting the fly down quickly into deep pockets in fast water. A weighted fly and leader are called for in these situations.

Casting weight is different from making your standard dry-fly cast. If you make a standard cast, you are likely to get tangles and maybe a big fly in your scalp. When using weight, cast by loading up the weight longer on the end of each cast. This means you hesitate longer at the end of each casting stroke and let the weight straighten out and actually tug on the rod before beginning the forward stroke. It's like a sling shot: you can't shoot it forward until you pull it back into a loaded position. Load the rod on each end and shoot as much line as you can between casting strokes.

The fewer false casts the better, so the lob cast is often used with heavy weight because it requires no false cast. When the current swings your fly around at the end of the drift, let the line straighten somewhat and point the rod tip at the fly. Then get the line moving with your line hand just before the forward stroke is done. The forward stroke is long and smooth

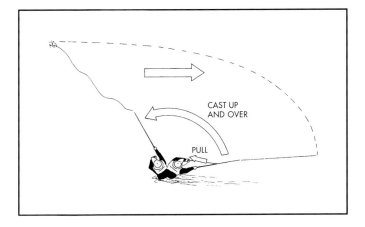

Lob Cast

and stops in the direction you want the fly to go. The drift is accomplished, and the lob cast is repeated. No back cast is ever made. This particular cast can save you lots of agony and increases the amount of time the fly is in the water where it is supposed to be.

When casting moderately or lightly weighted outfits and making a back cast, use a different technique. First get all the slack out of the line by pointing the rod tip at the flies and stripping in some line. Start the back cast by bringing the rod up quickly but smoothly to the side and then up at the back. Pick up a pencil and practice along with me. Point the pencil directly ahead. If you're right-handed, your wrist will cock to the right as the cast is started but will be pointed straight up and back at the completion of the back cast. Wait now! Let the weight curl out behind you and feel it almost tug on your rod, or pencil. As it loads up, bring the rod forward in a straight line. Stop the stroke at the normal position but allow the rod to continue drifting down. A rod left in an elevated position can get hit by the split-shot and become damaged. Repeat the

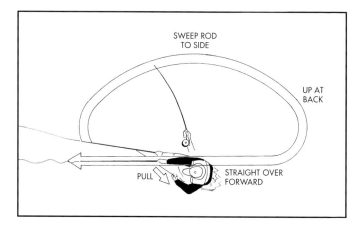

Oval Cast

process until the appropriate amount of line is out. If you do it properly, you seldom need more than one or two back casts, because a properly loaded cast shoots out well. Practice with the pencil several times and you will notice the tip goes round in a long oval, with a good hesitation at each end. This has been dubbed the "awful oval," but it's wonderful once you learn it properly. The most common mistake here is making the forward cast too soon. This flips the weights around the line and leader and causes tangles. If you're plagued by tangles, practice this cast and others listed in Lefty's casting books.

In Yellowstone Park and parts of Europe and in a few states where waterfowl are protected, lead fishing weights are illegal. This seems to be the trend, so get used to the idea of lead substitutes to sink your flies.

Lead as an underbody of the fly is legal in some waters where split-shot is not. Heavy wire can be used to weight flies and even small nymphs can be tied with wire thread instead of regular thread. Bead-head nymphs have steel, brass, or copper beads as weight. Steel or glass beads can be threaded onto your leaders and small pieces of toothpicks used to jam them in place. Put the beads on a dropper for ease of adding and subtracting weight. The steel and brass eyes now available can be substituted for lead-eye flies.

A lead substitute that is about 80 percent the weight of lead is being sold as non-toxic split-shot or "green" weight. Tin shot works but is hard and can damage leaders.

A fluorocarbon leader or Teflon-coated leader sinks much faster than monofilament and will get your nymphs down in shallow water. Use it as a part of your leader at least three feet away from the strike indicator, since it can sink small SIs. A section of lead-core trolling line can be included as part of the leader.

Experienced anglers of Atlantic salmon know another trick that has been used for centuries. Weighted flies are illegal on most salmon streams because they tend to become snagged. To get the fly down faster into deep water, a large, heavy hook is used with a small fly. The hook steel increases the weight, and the sparsely tied fly gets deeper. Heavy wire hooks are often enough weight in shallow waters.

Sinking lines were originally used in some nymphing techniques in streams but have largely been replaced by floating lines and strike indicators. They are still effective in some fast sections of rivers when fished with medium or large nymphs. (See "High-Stick Nymphing" later in the book.) Sinking lines are also effective with some streamer or nymph techniques.

In lakes, sinking lines become very valuable to nymphers. In some ponds, you can fish the shallows effectively with floating lines, long leaders, and weighted flies, but 90 percent of stillwater fishing is best done with sinking lines.

For most shallow, stillwater nymph applications, a Type I (slow-sinking) or Monocore ("slime") line is best. These lines sink slowly and allow you to count them down to the proper level before you start the retrieve. The lines will usually remain at about the same level while you retrieve slowly. Use these lines when fishing for shallow trout in ponds, in sloughs and weedbed channels, and during the damselfly-nymph migration. Faster sinking lines reach various depths so you should match them to trout feeding level or lake depth.

RIVER NYMPHING

Few people rig properly for nymphing. They set up once and never change. But adaptability is the key to nymphing success. This section will show how to rig and fish nymphing setups expertly. Just as casting and line manipulation help determine nymphing success, the business end of the leader has an often critical effect on consistent action. Since there are almost always trout feeding on nymphs, even during a hatch, nymphers should be catching trout throughout the day. If they aren't, their rigs are probably not set up properly.

Standard Strike-Indicator Nymphing

The standard strike-indicator system works everywhere and is the technique most commonly used for nymphing today. It is the most versatile and can be used with one or two subsurface flies in all but the deepest runs. It is also effective in stillwater.

The basic ingredients are a floating fly line, tapered leader (10 feet long, on average), and appropriately sized standard strike indicator, which is placed 1 1/2 to two times the depth of the water to be fished from the fly or flies. Attaching an SI too far from the flies will reduce reaction time for setting the hook. This is very important with educated fish. An SI that's too close won't allow the flies to sink into the strike zone. Properly rigged, the SI will support the fly's drift just off the bottom or at the feeding level of suspended fish.

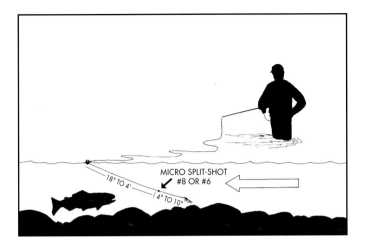

Shallow-Water Nymphing Rig

For nymphing in shallow water (six inches to two feet deep), place a small SI 18 inches to four feet from the fly. Little if any weight is used in water less than one foot deep. A #8 or #6 micro split-shot (1/16 to 1/8 inch in diameter) can be used in water up to two feet deep. Put the weight four to 10 inches from the fly. Use heavier weight and tippets and bigger SIs for shallow, pocket-water nymphing in rapids.

Most shallow-water nymphing is done in riffles, and you can approach fairly close to the trout if you wade cautiously, because they cannot see out through the choppy water very well. Use a small but colored SI that you can keep track of easily. Fish the water systematically and carefully. Trout in shallow water can miss your flies because their cone of vision is small. Several casts to each good-looking pocket are desirable. Change the angle of presentation regularly and leave no part of the shallows untried. You'll often be surprised by trout from very shallow water along the edges of riffles. Always fish the shallows before you wade in.

Line control in fast, shallow water is easier than it is in slow water. You're not casting far, and you can leave just a small amount of slack on the water and mend easily. A reach mend during the cast is often all that is needed. Small amounts of drag are masked by the choppy currents. Wiggle line out for a longer drift.

Use shallow-water rigs in deep, slow water where trout are suspended close to the surface — in back eddies or slow current areas, for example. A white, light pink, or dry-fly indicator that blends in well with surface foam is recommended. It will be harder to see but will distract selective fish much less than a more visible SI. Let the unweighted or lightly weighted flies drift around with the slow water, and watch the SI closely for the slightest of twitches. Remember, the flies are shallow in deeper water here and any bump will be a trout. If your indicator is not drifting exactly like the bubbles on top, improve the drift by introducing more slack line. Unnatural drift is easily seen by the trout and avoided.

Trout on the shallow flats and tailouts of runs are the toughest to approach because they are unprotected and spooky. You must sneak up slowly, perhaps on your knees, and cast carefully with the smallest indicator and lightest tippets you can manage. The greased-leader technique described later works well here. Excessive mending will spook the fish, so mend well above the trout's position and allow plenty of slack as the flies go by the trout. If the flies start dragging near the trout, just let the flies swing below and try again. Mending on top of spooky trout is counterproductive. Set the hook gently if a take is perceived; tight tippets and spooky trout don't like noisy hooksets. If you consistently catch selective trout on nymphs in this type of water, you are one of a lucky few.

In weedy spring creeks, use a shallow-water rig to drift small nymphs in the channels between the weedbeds and the drop-offs behind weed clusters. Work for accuracy and maximum depth in the weedy channels. The dry-fly indicator technique with a dropper nymph also does quite well.

The average strike-indicator rig that is most frequently used in streams has a 10-foot leader and an SI placed five to 10 feet from the fly, which is tied to a tippet of the proper pound-test or X-rating. To figure out the correct X-rating of a tippet, try dividing the hook size by three. For example, a #12 hook would require a 4X-tippet. (See table.) I seldom go below 5X-tippet for nymphing. There are times when 6X is a necessity for super-selective trout in clear, shallow water, but I like to use the heaviest tippet I can get away with. Don't let your tackle take the place of presentation skill. The lighter the tippet, the longer you must play hooked fish, and this increases your chance of exhausting the trout.

TIPPET	FLY PATTERN	WATER PROFILE	TROUT PROFILE
6X	#16 to #28 flies	slow and clear	selective, 6" to 18"
5X	#14 to #20 nymphs	pond or stream	educated, 8" to 20"
4X	#10 to #18 nymphs	pond or river	12" to 22"
3X	#6 to #12 nymphs	fast or stillwater	14" to 28" or uneducated
2X	#4 to #10 flies	fast, or big lake	16" to 30"
1X	#2 to #6 stoneflies crayfish	fast or snag-filled	18" to 32"
0X	#1 to #6 nymphs	fast or very snag-filled	20" to 36"

Note: Recommendations are for optimum playing time.
Tippets are capable of catching larger trout than indicated.

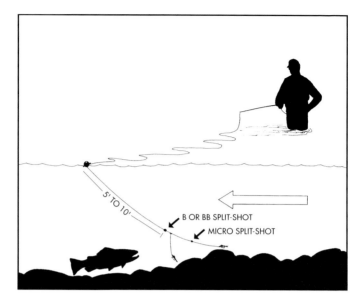

Standard Nymphing Rig

I like to use two flies at once because they give the fish a choice and allow you to try out more patterns faster. The rig is easily made by leaving one end of your tippet knot (Blood Knot or Triple Surgeon's Knot) long and tying on another fly. The main weight is placed above the dropper, and a micro split-shot is often used near the bottom fly to ensure that it stays down. Some states such as Alaska do not allow two-fly rigs. Check local regulations.

This rig works well in the deeper riffles, runs, rapids, and some pools, 2 1/2 to six feet deep. One B or BB split-shot placed above the dropper fly will get the unweighted or lightly weighted fly down. If the fly is unweighted, use a micro split-shot close to the bottom fly.

Strike indicators should be medium-sized or large. They should be pink, bright red, or orange if the water is fast and choppy, and white or chartreuse if the water is slow. Yarn in-dicators are popular with some anglers. Just attach a piece of Glo-Bug-type tow yarn by putting it in a slip knot in the leader. Grease up the yarn with fly floatant and trim it to the desired size. Big, highly visible indicators like this work well — if you can cast them. (They are more wind-resistant.)

It is important to be able to move the SI up or down the leader as the water type and depth change. Long distances between the SI and the fly in shallow water will sometimes make strike detection difficult. Too short a distance means the flies can't get to the bottom. If the leader is long enough but the flies are not getting down, add weight until you start touch-ing bottom on most casts. If the fly is snagging the bottom too often, lighten up or reduce the SI distance. Keeping the SI rig adapted to the water you are fishing will likely double your hookup rates.

Mending and slack control with this rig can mean the dif-ference between a two-fish day and a 25-fish day. Two anglers, each fishing the same rig with the same flies, can have that much difference in success. I can't stress enough the impor-tance of a natural, drag-free drift. If you don't do reach casts and mends and don't introduce slack, you are dragging too much for many fish. Look at your line during the drift. If you consistently have one big belly or one big "S"-curve, you have drag and need to work on presentation.

You want to achieve numerous "S"-curves in the line to allow the terminal nymph rig to stay put in the slower cur-rent near the stream bottom. If your flies get down to the slower water along the bottom, the SI on the surface will slow perceptibly and you'll know you're in the strike zone. Any-time your SI is going even slightly faster than the current, your drift is unacceptable.

Sometimes you simply need to change your casting posi-tion. If you're casting across slow water to faster water, try to get closer to the fast water so that your line doesn't drag on the slow. A good nympher has his rod in constant motion, mending, wiggling slack out, and reaching to get a few more inches out of a good drift. If you become bored nymphing, you're doing it wrong. Concentrate on each aspect of casting, mending, line manipulation, and strike detection.

When nymphing power water (deep, swift, big currents), you can lengthen the leader considerably by adding long tippets, up to 18 feet from SI to fly. The power-water rig is difficult to use but quite effective for big fish. You must make long casts and big mends and have considerable line-control skill to get the long drifts needed. Big SIs are the rule for supporting a weighted fly and weighted leader in heavy water.

Use your regular tapered leader but add a length of tippet. The long tippet curls out terribly but the advantages on the

Deep, Fast-Water Nymphing Rig

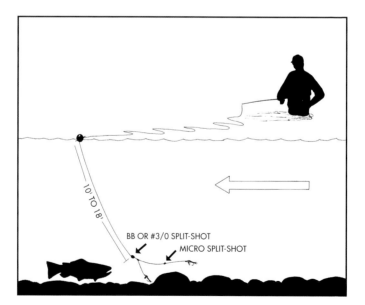

10' TO 18'

BB OR #3/0 SPLIT-SHOT

MICRO SPLIT-SHOT

water make the effort worthwhile. Long tippets sink faster than the thick part of the tapered leader, so less weight is needed. The fly also often lands in a pile, helpful in nymphing. The best nymphers commonly use what's called a "tuck cast" to ensure lots of slack right under the indicator for fast sink rates.

The tuck cast is done by stopping the nymph rod high up during the cast so the weight swings around quickly at the end, bounces back a little, and dives down into the water first, right under the SI. The flies then sink straight down quickly rather than being cast straight and having to cut through the water the entire length of the leader.

It's the only way to get down fast without loads of weight. This technique is valuable for any nymphing rig but almost a necessity for power-water nymphing. I'm not going to kid you: few people do this type of nymphing, because it's lots of work. So there are often large trout living in deep water with a strong current. The biggest trout are frequently right down at the base of the gnarliest, nastiest water, with their nose against a rock. They can sit there for months and feed and never even see a fly presented properly to them.

I recall one such fish from the Henry's Fork in Idaho. This Box Canyon rainbow weighed 7 3/4 pounds but was only 22 inches long. It had been just sitting there behind a rock in the rapids, eating like a pig, until a nymph was drifted right over the lip of that rock and down to its feeding level. Hundreds of nymphs had drifted over it too high, but only a rare one got to the right depth.

A clean, high-floating line is required for mending at distances. Try a roll mend. Practice a roll cast until you have it down, then combine the roll cast with an upstream mend. Roll the line right up to the SI and upstream. Sometimes two mends are required back to back, then slack is fed out the rod tip for a long drift. Long casts and long drifts are necessary to allow time for the nymphs to reach their primary target.

Once your nymph is there, you want it to stay in that area for as long as possible. If you can mend the line so that most of it is upstream of the indicator, then feed out line. You can often get a drift 20 to 70 feet long down in the strike zone. Most nymphers might get the fly down for two or seven feet, but then drag brings it back up. Just by keeping it down there you have greatly increased your chances. Selective fish will often watch a nymph coming toward them, and if they notice any unnatural drag they will reject it. If the fish is unsure, it may drift back with the fly, watching to see if it looks wrong. If the fly keeps drifting naturally, the fish will often turn and attack it before it leaves the fish's home water. Since most flies will start swinging up, the fish is conditioned to wait for a long, natural drift before acceptance. This is true with all stream nymphing rigs, not just power-water rigs.

If you make long casts, use long leaders and weighted flies, and have good line-manipulation technique, you can reach some of these monsters lurking in big, deep rivers. No sinking line will get your fly down faster than this rig and technique. These situations are also where nymphing and streamer fishing mix. Streamers can be fished in the same way, and as the patterns roll down the bottom currents, big, opportunistic trout will take notice.

To set the hook with a long cast and lots of slack, you must use the current. Always set the hook with the rod low and parallel to the water. This allows the water tension to help and keeps tension on a trout that is lightly hooked until slack can be stripped in and the hook reset. Finding the right balance between too much and too little slack in a drifting line is a real challenge, and setting the hook can be, too. I almost always set the hook downstream. The nymph slips into the corner of the trout's jaw and finds a good spot for the hook. Setting downstream increases hookups with any nymphing, dry-fly, or streamer rig. Give it a try.

Sometimes a downstream, sidearm hookset is out. In these cases, it is almost as effective to set the hook upstream with a very low rod angle. The water tension can still help. If you were to raise the rod straight up to set the hook, you might have to move too much slack, and you'll miss some fish.

Although big nymphs are the rule in power water, sometimes trout from deep runs want small flies. I recall a 12-foot-deep run on a large Montana river where the trout were feeding on mayfly and caddis nymphs. With a deep-water rig and some small nymphs, I was able to get numerous fish. They were obviously feeding with abandon because they thought they were safe.

One variation is to use streamers on this nymphing rig. Streamers have accounted for some very big trout but are seldom used that way by anglers. Everything in the rig is the same but a Woolly Bugger, Muddler Minnow, Strymph, or similar, buggy pattern is used instead of a standard nymph. With streamer-type patterns, frequent mends up or downstream often twitch the fly tantalizingly along the bottom. I like lead-eye flies with this rig. Fish the fly on the swing at the bottom of the drift as well.

Using any of these rigs from drift boats is easy. Only the angle of presentation is different. Instead of casting up and across, cast across or even slightly downstream of your position and immediately mend the line and put the right amount of slack on the water. Make occasional adjustments to the slack, and you can get a long drift.

Dry-Fly-Indicator Nymphing

One of the most pleasant and effective ways to nymph is to use a dry fly as a strike indicator, with a nymph hanging underneath. This blends the best of both worlds — dry flies and nymphs. Although the dry fly usually takes a back seat to the nymph, it plays an integral role. This rig is a synergism

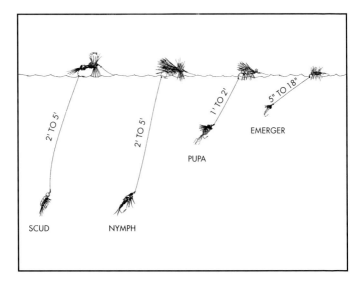

Dry-Fly Indicator Rigs

of sorts, like 1+1=11 instead of 2. No nymphing rig is more effective in water where the fish are feeding selectively within three or four feet of the surface. The indicator is not a bulb of flashy color; it's more natural and can be changed as many times as there are dry-fly patterns. The trout never get used to it the way they can with standard indicators.

The basic rig is a dry fly tied to the end of a seven to nine-foot tapered leader. A length of tippet is then tied to the bend of the dry or to the eye of the dry fly. The tippet end receives a nymph or another subsurface imitation. The dry fly can be anything from a #22 midge to a #2 bucktail dry fly, but it should complement the sunken fly. For example, a #18 may-fly dry could be paired with a #18 Pheasant Tail Nymph, or a big Trude dry could be paired with a stonefly nymph. But a large stonefly nymph would easily sink a small mayfly dry almost immediately. Big dry flies with small nymphs and micro split-shot are perfectly acceptable. There are almost limitless combinations possible.

If the dry fly has enough flotation, the dropper nymph or tippet can be weighted lightly. The tippet can be anywhere from five inches to five feet long. Match the feeding level of the fish. Get the nymph to the bottom unless fish are cruising under scum lines or else suspended, watching for hatch-bound nymphs or emergers near the surface.

One value of the dry-fly system is that opportunistic fish often take the dry fly as well. More often, the dry fly catches a trout's attention and the fish investigates. The trout often rejects the dry, but as it turns away it sees the nymph and takes it, almost as if to make the effort worthwhile. This often happens with attractor dries paired with small, natural nymphs. Synergism.

Fish a dry-indicator rig in riffles, quiet currents, stillwater, pocket water, and along shore. It works particularly well for suspended fish feeding under a scum line in an eddy. The water may be 10 feet deep, but the trout are up feeding on the conveyor belt full of food.

This combination also works very well from drift boats or rafts, and it gives two differently feeding trout a choice. When trout are very aggressive — when their strike zones are big — the dry fly gets hit as frequently as the nymph, but normally the nymph gets taken about three times as often.

Riffles and shallow runs are natural spots to try. Because many of the hatches originate here, a combination of adult insect and nymph or emerger is often deadly. One of my favorite combos is an Elk-Hair Caddis paired with a LaFontaine Sparkle Pupa. It can be fished natural-drift, and at the end of the drift, the fly is swung up in the current. The rig can be twitched and skittered on the surface, then the rod dropped and the flies left to drift some more. It imitates well the fast ascent of the pupa and the dancing egg-laying of the adult.

Caddis hatches are one of the few times where highly active nymph movements are effective.

Spring creeks are overlooked by many nymphers. The weedbeds continually catch nymphs fished with standard rigs, but the small nymph fished suspended under a small dry fly can really provide some hot action. I've seen trout nail the little suspended nymphs one cast after another when even the best dry-fly presentations were met with disdain.

This two-fly rig can be fished as you would a dry-fly rig. Just work your way up a run, casting to likely spots. Dragless drifts are just as important here as with any other natural-drift techniques. Watch the dry fly as you would a strike indicator. If it suddenly disappears, set the hook — a trout is on the nymph. This is very exciting when trout are in the shallows. From drift crafts, just cast toward the bank or toward some other good-looking trout water, and get long drifts.

Greased-Leader Nymphing

When little midges or emerging mayfly nymphs are moving in slow water, the greased-leader technique works well. It won't work in riffles or rapids because you must be able to see the leader track on a slick surface. It is a great technique for flats, slicks, tailouts, and some back eddies.

The rig is just your normal floating line and tapered leader with a small nymph or emerger attached. You add no SI but you do grease up the leader with fly floatant to several inches from the fly for emergers and to two or three feet from the fly with nymphs. Once greased up, the leader floats high in the surface film, not breaking surface tension but depressing it. The leader track is highly visible in the right light and can be watched as you would watch a standard SI. When the leader track twitches or sinks quickly, set the hook.

You cannot use weighted leaders or flies, so this is mainly a technique for fishing a fly within 18 inches of the surface.

You can make a light presentation and spook fewer trout in shallow, flat water with this rig. When casting to slick-water trout, remember to false cast away from the fish. False casting over spooky trout will put them down.

This rig also works in stillwater situations where the surface is calm and trout are feeding shallow on midges or mayflies. Standard nymphs on this rig can be fished in any water, but without an SI you will miss many hits.

Bounce Nymphing

Bounce nymphing has been around for a while, but it has mainly been used by a few old-timers who originally fished bait with fly rods in streams and who now fish flies the same way. Some progressive anglers and I have taken this technique a step further and have found it to be a great trout producer in a variety of waters.

Bounce nymphing doesn't work everywhere, but most of you can find some waters where it will. It is best used in medium-fast to fast current in gravelly areas like riffles, runs, and rapids one to six feet deep. It's a poor rig for weedy areas or where there are many big, jagged rocks, but in the right water type, watch out! It's amazing to see how it can vacuum feeding trout from a run.

The rig is the most involved of any discussed in this book, but it developed from a simple idea: keeping the nymphs just up off the bottom for as long as possible. Sound familiar? What is different in bounce nymphing is that the weight is placed on the very end of the leader and the flies are tied to droppers above the weights.

Start with about a seven-foot tapered leader on your floating line, and add four to six feet of 3X to 6X-tippet material. Now you'll need one or two droppers. Fold the last 1 1/2 to two feet over and tie a big Double or Triple Surgeon's Loop there. Cut the loop open three to six inches from the knot and you have one dropper. Repeat the process 10 to 12 inches down from the first dropper knot to end up with two droppers that don't touch while they hang, and an eight to 14-inch tag end at the bottom. The finished rig is like a capital "F" attached to your leader.

Put the SI on the leader near the end of the fly line. Unlike regular nymphing rigs, the SI is placed at a distance three or four times the water depth from the flies. Tie an Overhand Knot on the bottom of the "F" and attach a BB or #3/0 split-shot to the end. Tie on two small nymphs, scuds, San Juan Worms, or egg patterns. This rig works particularly well with the small nymphs that selective trout like to feed on; big or weighted nymphs snag the bottom too often. The typical bounce rig is about six to 14 feet from SI to weights. The SI should be fairly large to stay on the surface as the weights bounce the bottom.

Weights heavier than usual and long, supple leaders make standard false casting difficult and dangerous with this rig. Use the lob cast described earlier so that no back cast is necessary. The sinkers will hit the bottom quickly and start bouncing over the gravel. You will see the rhythmic twitching of the indicator, which is going slower than the current, as the weights bounce downstream.

Line control is a little different here. Without a belly in the fly line, the weights would continually stop the rig in all but the fastest water. Let a small belly develop in the line after the nymphs reach bottom, and mend the rest upstream. The water pressure on the belly counteracts the resistance of the weights, and the flies drift and bounce along just above the bottom. Adjust the size of the belly to regulate the nymphs' speed. Use a small belly for slow fly speed and a big belly or lighter weights when the flies are stopping too often.

It sounds like a wild and crazy technique but it works extremely well in the right water types. The flies are in the strike

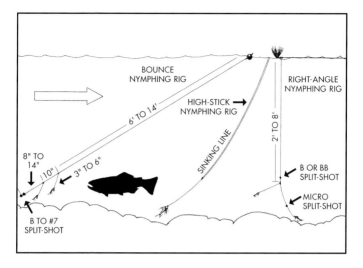

Bounce, High-Stick, and Right-Angle Nymphing Rigs

zone as much as five to 10 times longer than the flies of a standard indicator rig. When you keep the flies down in the strike zone that long, you are bound to interest more trout.

Some people use a 1-weight fly line on a rod of their choice. Since the line is not a major factor in a lob cast, a 1 or 2-weight line works fine on a 4 to 7-weight rod. The finer diameter of the light line is better for regulating the fly-drift speed, and less weight is needed. A few people use monofilament line instead of fly line. It works well but doesn't give the feel and mending control of fly line.

This technique is called "the bounce" for obvious reasons — you'll see the indicator bouncing along in the current. You'll then suddenly notice a different kind of hesitation and the hook will set. Because there is a tight line between the indicator and the weights, the small nymphs normally used with this rig will almost set the hook themselves. Few fish are missed in bounce nymphing.

Feeding fish are interested when this technique is used because it delivers the nymphs at the right level, or two different levels when you use two droppers. It also seems to wake up non-feeding fish. I think they can feel the weights bouncing down toward them, and because the flies meet the fish at nose level, a fish would rather open its mouth and take the fly than move out of the way. Give it a try in a trout-laden riffle or run, and I believe you will be convinced that it is one of the best nymphing techniques there is.

Right-Angle Nymphing

Right-angle nymphing is fishing a drifting nymph at a 90-degree angle. The fly is straight below the SI, not trailing behind, and this makes the rig sensitive to light takes. To set up, place a half-hitch over the toothpick on the bottom of a standard SI rig. The half-hitch creates a roughly 90-degree bend in the leader which straightens out during casting. However, keep in mind that presentation technique is as important for this setup as the rig itself. Right-angle nymphing works best in long runs of even depth.

It is often done using a big yarn indicator. The yarn is tied to the end of a four to seven-foot tapered leader using a Clinch Knot. The two to eight-foot tippet is tied to the leader, just behind the yarn indicator, with another Clinch Knot. The long tippet sinks quickly, and added weight is used if needed. The tippet is lengthened or shortened as water depths change. (See illustration on page 101.)

This rig is best used with a tuck cast or a trailing-fly cast. Ideally, you let the fly land first, with a tuck cast, and the leader and indicator pile up right on top of the nymph. The nymph then quickly sinks straight down.

The trailing-fly cast is done a bit like a puddle cast. Actually, it almost looks like an aborted cast, where the flies never turn over or straighten out at the end. Since the leader never turns over, it drops to the surface with lots of slack and the fly sinks quickly.

Begin by making a puddle cast, which is a cast that goes up at both ends but with the rod low at the center — a "U"-shaped cast. On a normal puddle cast, the dry fly straightens out and bounces back and the leader piles up on itself, creating lots of drag-fighting slack. With a weighted nymph and wind-resistant yarn indicator, however, the flies can be puddle-cast but the heavy, wind-resistant nymphs skim the surface and drop to the water first, without turning over. The end of the fly line often lands past the SI and nymph, creating some good slack.

The trailing-fly cast takes practice to control, but you'll be learning how to make a nymphing cast with lots of slack. The cast has a number of subtle variations and requires almost

Trailing-Fly Cast

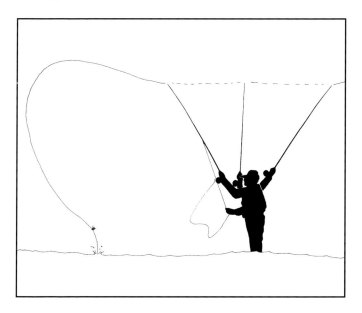

immediate mending to position the slack in the ideal location. It's a cast that becomes more effective the more skilled you become at subtle presentation techniques and mends. Long, natural drifts are possible with the nymphs suspended in the strike zone. This technique has been used for steelhead with great success as well, because the fly can be suspended at or just above the steelhead's level.

High-Stick Nymphing

High-stick nymphing is a traditional technique which was made popular by Charlie Brooks in his writings. It still works in many fast-water areas but has been largely replaced by SI techniques. The technique is as implied by its name. The rod is held high and the nymphs are drifted through the water in front of the angler, who should try to feel what is happening while getting as natural a drift as possible. The technique works well up close in fast water but is difficult on long casts because the current creates too much drag and makes strike detection difficult. In slow water, the tight line between high rod and flies causes too much drag for selective trout.

High-stick nymphing is best suited for fast riffles, rapids, and pocket water, especially when done with heavily weighted flies and leaders. Fast-sinking lines and short, stout leaders are common. (See illustration on page 101.) With floating lines use a nine or 10-foot leader and enough weight to get the flies down in fast water.

First make a lob cast upstream. Allow enough time for the flies to reach the bottom strike zone, then raise the rod to control the flies' drift. Don't drag the fly if you can avoid it. Keep just sufficient tension in the line so that you are able to feel the fly stopping on a rock or at a fish's mouth. The rod starts out low, and shortly after the cast it is raised gradually, passing the angler's position at the rod's highest level. It is then lowered as it drifts downstream.

In places where trout don't mind some drag, this technique works well. If fish are very drift-conscious, use a standard SI rig. High-stick nymphing is a very good technique for some crossover patterns, such as streamers which are fished on a nymphing rig. The slight drag causes the streamer to appear active while it rolls and tumbles along the bottom. It also works very well in Alaska when big trout are feeding on salmon fry in early summer or are eating salmon flesh. It is a cross between natural-drift nymphing and a wet-fly swing.

You can mend up or down to get the fly to swim upstream or downstream. It is popular to mend downstream, feed line out once the big nymphs reach the bottom, and then swing the fly up at the end of the drift. It works well for uneducated, wild fish or for trout in early season during high water.

A variation is the Leisenring Lift. Everything is the same except that the rod is lightly pumped up and down during the drift in order to raise and lower the fly in the water column. This technique works with caddis larvae and pupae, stonefly nymphs, and streamers.

Spin-Rod Nymphing

Why spin-rod nymphing in a fly-fishing book? Some anglers cannot cast and mend fly lines properly. Kids too young to handle a fly rod can be rigged up with a spin rod. Some older anglers cannot cast the weighted nymph rig for long, and some physically or mentally challenged people can use a spin rod but not a fly rod. The techniques that follow make it possible to fly fish with easy-to-use tackle. Many states allow spinning tackle even in fly-only waters. However, "fly only" in some states means just flies, fly rod, fly line, and fly reel. Check local fly-fishing definitions to be sure.

There are times and places where not even the most experienced nymphers can reach and properly nymph some water types. These are the situations where a spin rod and nymphs are ideal. Deep riffles, big, fast runs, the holes below rapids, and typical but swift nymphing runs are all easily fished with this particular rig. Most nymphers know of some water where the depth and power of the water, the distance of the cast, or the drift required is virtually impossible for traditional fly tackle. Spinning tackle can solve some presentation problems for nymphers, if they can get past the stigma that snooty fly flingers have attached to it.

Bounce nymphing can be done with spinning tackle, and this is the most effective way to nymph the distant power water that frustrates regular nymphing. In fact, it works best in the waters where other nymphers cannot fish properly. It fills a gap left in nymphing presentation techniques.

The basic rig is a long, light spin rod six to eight feet long (or a spin reel on a fly rod), rated for 1 to 8-pound-test line. It should have a light or ultra-light action, stiff butt, and sensitive tip. The reel can be a closed or open-face spinning reel, one that is designed for 1 to 8-pound line and has a good, smooth drag. Four or 6-pound-test lines are normally used. The terminal end is built the same as it is on a fly-rod bouncing rig, with the weights at the bottom and one or two droppers above the weights. An SI is not used, except in some shallow water situations where there is not enough current to work the system properly (and usually a regular fly outfit would work better in those situations anyway). Most of the time no SI or bobber is used in spin-rod nymphing.

The weights can be anything from one BB split-shot to several #7 cannonball weights. I like to use removable shot because you need to adjust the weight to each run, but round weights snag up less. Non-lead weights can be used as well.

The flies usually best for spin-rod nymphing are under #10, right down to #22s, but larger flies such as stonefly nymphs can be used if unweighted. Do not use weighted nymph patterns, since they will hang up too often.

Cast up and across into the top of a good-looking power run. Click the bail over and let the weights sink right to the bottom. Raise the rod to a high angle (perpendicular to the line) so that you can feel the weights bouncing along the rocky bottom. A sandy or muddy bottom is okay, but not weeds. Most fast water has a rocky bottom anyway. If you cast almost straight upstream, you must reel in the slack as it comes back to you in the current. Casts made across but just slightly upstream need no reeling of slack; just hold the rod high.

Always try to imagine the nymphs drifting at the same speed as the currents along the bottom, and in a straight line, not swinging. The typical cast is up and across at a 45-degree angle. A few turns of the reel are made to collect some slack and then the weights are allowed to bounce the rest of the way. The current will bow the line, which is fine, but do not allow too much slack, or setting the hook will be a problem.

Spin-Rod Nymphing Rigs

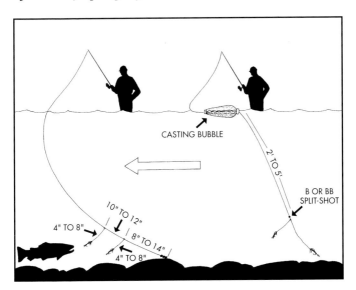

CASTING BUBBLE

2' TO 5'

B OR BB
SPLIT-SHOT

10" TO 12"

4" TO 8"

8" TO 14"

4" TO 8"

Raise the rod to a vertical position as it passes you and then lower it slowly as it passes downstream. If you reel too much, it will drag the flies unnaturally and shorten the natural bounce and drift considerably.

Strikes are partly felt and partly seen. Watch the line where it enters the water. If it stops or shoots upstream, set the hook. Some trout hook themselves, but some hits are very light. Set the hook on everything that feels or looks unnatural, until you can tell the difference between the bottom and a fish.

Another spin-rod technique employs a fly and bubble, in larger rivers or on stillwater. Any spinning tackle can be used. A special plastic bobber is filled with water to provide casting weight and to stay at the desired drift level. (See illustration on page 107.) Some bobbers have surgical tubing running through the center; the tubing can be twisted, trapping the line. Others just have a hole, so a swivel is placed three to five feet from the fly to keep the bubble from slipping down.

In rivers, the bubble is usually half to three-quarters full of water to make it float. A small weight is added above the nymph so it will sink to the desired depth. Cast up and across-stream and let the bubble drift naturally with the current.

In lakes, leave some air in the bubble to fish it right in the surface film; this is a good technique to apply when fish are rising regularly. Otherwise, fill the bubble completely and maybe add a weight right at the bubble. Count the bubble down just as you would a sinking fly line. Retrieve the bubble and the fly slowly with occasional pauses.

STILLWATER NYMPHING

Stillwater nymphing requires a whole different mindset. The currents in lakes are generally too slow for using standard natural-drift techniques. The angler must give the fly action so that it interests cruising trout. Trout in stillwater are continually swimming forward instead of swimming relatively stationary against the current. Besides the different trout habits and foods, the angler must relate completely differently to the trout environment. Instead of wading up a river, you must learn how to control small watercraft or stalk cruising fish.

Stillwater nymphing may not have the same allure as nymphing in running water, but it can become completely intriguing just the same. Many stillwaters are beautiful and hold very large trout, many more than in streams. Learning how to nymph stillwaters will also get you away from streams during crowded periods. I never feel as crowded fishing in a lake as I do in a busy river. This type of nymphing appeals to the solitary side of fly fishing. And knowing that the big one might hit on the next cast keeps the senses alert.

Stillwater Watercraft

About 80 percent of stillwater fly fishing is done from some type of watercraft, for obvious reasons. Many lakes are too deep to wade, and too muddy or weedy in the places where you can touch bottom.

Float tubes and U-tubes are used with fins and are common among lake fly fishers. They work well for positioning yourself in small bays and ponds and they are relatively low-profile and inexpensive ($50 to $300). On the downside, you are sitting low in the water and can get cold easily, and they are difficult to kick around, cast from, or spot trout from over distances. They are almost impossible to take through weedbeds, where your legs and fins get tangled.

Kick boats are bigger and often allow you to sit above the water. Casting, spotting fish, speed, and control options are all positive. Electric motors, oars, or fins can be used for propulsion. Small pontoons are fine for stillwater use and have about as little wind drag as float tubes. Bigger models can be used on some rivers and let you sit higher and cast farther, but they are more affected by the wind. Control is easy once you learn how to keep the wind at your back and cast downwind. They run $200 to $1000 or more. While costlier and generally heavier than float tubes, they are still much cheaper than boats and much more portable. They are faster than float tubes and can carry more gear. Many stillwater anglers are finding these boats ideal for stillwaters, especially where no motors are allowed.

Boats are comfortable to fish from but the most difficult to control. A boat often must be anchored to keep the wind from drifting you away from prime water. But drifting with the wind in a boat while dragging a fly can be very productive for finding concentrations of trout. Just motor to the upwind end of a bay and fish as you drift, then motor back to the top of the wind drift. A drift sock can slow your speed in moderate or stiff winds. You can wind-drift in float tubes or kick boats but they are harder to get back upwind unless motorized.

Canoes are good for smaller, protected waters and slow rivers but are hard to control in the wind. Unless anchored, they are best maneuvered by one person while the other fishes.

Finding the Trout

One of the reasons fly rodders often overlook stillwater fisheries is that you cannot read a trout lake the way you can a stream. Finding the fish in a large piece of water may seem a challenge. Trout in lakes cruise feeding lanes. The food in lakes is not evenly distributed and neither are the trout.

Much of the food is concentrated in the littoral zone, shallows that receive lots of sunshine and often have many weedbeds. The shallows of a lake are the real food producers. Anglers regularly avoid weedbeds, thinking that the trout in lakes are fish of the open water. While trout often pass through the deeper areas and you can catch some fish there, most of their feeding is done in the littoral zone or the sublittoral zone, the transition from the shallows to deeper water. Avoiding the cruising lanes in weedbeds is counterproductive.

So instead of casting blindly to deep water, you have some structure to fish, which cuts down on your search. Trout are often more structure-oriented than we believe. They do not hold to tight cover to ambush prey as pike or bass do, but they do cruise cover looking for their foods, which are most plentiful in areas of some cover.

The deep water where light and oxygen do not regularly reach is known as the *profundal zone*. Few if any fish live there, but in the surface layers above, trout may feed on clouds of daphnia or follow baitfish in the open water. Finding those fish may just be chance, but finding feeding lanes is fairly easy.

One way to find trout in open water is to troll flies from a tube or a boat, an old technique that still works. Troll with fins, a small motor, oars, a paddle, or with the wind. Adjust your speed from fast to very slow. Once a fish is hooked, search the area more thoroughly by stopping and casting in a pattern around you.

If it's windy, or if you think it will be hard to stay in the same vicinity, throw out a marker. Markers are foam blocks with string and a weight attached. Just throw the marker out and let the string unwind from the block. It will stop automatically when the weight hits bottom, marking your spot for future reference. Fish a pattern around the marker, and once you're satisfied that you've worked the water properly, pick up the marker and move on.

When wind-drifting in a big bay, drop a marker over when you hook a fish, then continue drifting. If action gets better, drop another marker. Once action slows, motor or row back upwind and anchor the boat near the markers. These will often prove to be where trout are concentrated. This technique is especially useful in big bays that average less than 20 feet deep.

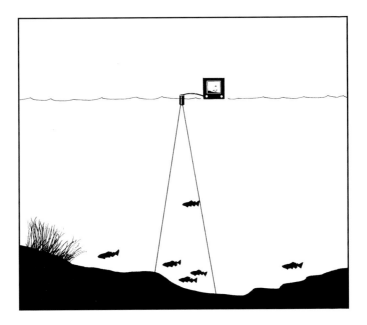

Fishfinder

Electronic fishfinders allow you to learn the bottom structure of bays and points so that you can read trout cruising lanes in deeper water. Some people feel this is cheating and is unfair to the trout. You won't think so when the fishfinder shows fish all around you and you can't catch them. Fishfinders help you to learn a piece of stillwater faster than any other method I know.

Casting haphazardly to open water is a case of hit-or-miss and you learn little about the water. The fishfinder is another source of information. It's common to be going over a shallow weedbed and then suddenly have a hit as you find a drop-off. Often the drop-off is only a few feet deeper, but it is an important feeding lane for the trout and something you would not have found without the fishfinder.

When you learn how to read the fishfinder, you can tell the difference between weedbeds, rocky bottom, and muddy bottom. The transducer shoots a signal straight down which bounces off the bottom and comes back to the finder, where it's seen on a screen. The transducer cone is usually narrow, about a 17 to 20-degree cone. It won't show much but the bottom in shallow water but will let you learn how lake structure relates to number of fish hit.

One recent development in fish-finding technology is the sidefinder. This device shoots a signal to the side rather than simply straight down. When trout are shallow, they can be seen on the sidefinder. You can rotate the sidefinder slowly and find trout out to the side. Because these are shallow trout, it is not difficult to present a fly to them. A sidefinder makes the task of finding concentrations of fish much easier, and if you lose them, you can just rotate the transducer again and determine which direction they are heading.

Sidefinder

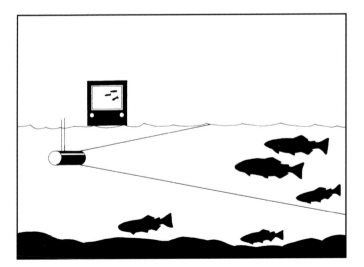

A small, self-contained unit made by Bottom Line, called the "Fishing Buddy II," has proven to be the ideal sonar for stillwater fly fishers. It has both side and down-aiming transducers built in and shows both findings simultaneously. Remember, it only shows you the bottom and perhaps where the fish are. You still have to learn how to catch them.

Lake Lines and Methods

Sinking lines are the lake angler's best tool. An angler who only occasionally fishes stillwater may try his floating fly line in stillwater but with limited success. We've already discussed fly-presentation level, so you know how important that can be. The right fly-line sink rate is what gets you to the right level in lakes.

Sinking fly lines generally cast and shoot more easily than floating fly lines. The finer diameter of sinking lines cuts through the wind and shoots through the guides better. Although floating lines are used in some shallow-water techniques, sinking lines are employed by typical lake nymphers approximately 90 percent of the time.

Retrieves are plentiful and vary greatly. But the rod tip should always be pointed straight down the fly line, even if this means putting the rod tip underwater during the retrieve. You want a tight line between the fly and the stripping finger on your rod hand. That way you can feel every bump and tug. A good nympher who's concentrating can feel the fly brush some aquatic vegetation and can tell the difference between that and a trout's take.

Setting the hook is done slowly. If you set the hook too fast you'll miss many trout, especially with tailed flies like Woolly Buggers. Wait for the solid pull, like a rubber band stretching, before you set the hook. Usually all you need to do is lift the rod, not rip it all the way up. The water tension on the sinking line helps set the hook. Keep your hooks sharp.

Extra-fast-sinking (Type VI) lines and lead-core shooting tapers are designed to get down fast and stay there. They are not used much for nymphing except in clear, deep lakes where you need to present the fly to fish cruising 15 to more than 30 feet deep. They are mostly used to fish big minnow flies deep and fast. Fly control and strike detection at these depths are difficult but possible. Some people fish these lines for big trout in big lakes, where action is usually slow but the rewards may be great. Some lakes have no oxygen below 30 feet, so no trout will be there.

Extra-fast-sinking lines (Type IV or V) are used to keep your flies down on fast retrieves in moderate to deep water (10 to 20 feet deep). Again, they are rarely used for stillwater nymphing but will fish the depths with crayfish, minnow, and leech patterns. These lines are good for high-stick nymphing in fast water with large nymphs.

Fast-sinking lines (Type III) are entering the nympher's realm. These lines are good for fishing leeches, crayfish, dragonfly nymphs, and streamers. They work well with medium and fast retrieves in the 10 to 18-foot depths common in the deeper bays of lakes and reservoirs. When surface waters are warm, the trout head for the deep water close to weedbeds or rocky points where they can feed.

On slow retrieves (one to five inches a second), the fast-sinking line keeps sinking. When you retrieve faster (six to 18 inches a second), the line stays at about the same depth as when the stripping began. Fish the deepest weedbeds and the edges of deep-water drop-offs. The line works in shallow water only on fast retrieves. It works reasonably well for searching big water with fast retrieves and bigger flies (such as Woolly Buggers, dragonfly nymphs, and streamers). A typical retrieve with this line is an eight to 18-inch strip every second or two. Fishing fast will find opportunistic fish and sometimes make big trout hit when they wouldn't on a slower retrieve.

The medium-sinking (Type II) fly line is the stillwater nympher's mainstay. If you have only one fly line to use for stillwater, it should be this one. It can be fished effectively in three to 17 feet of water — littoral and sublittoral zones in most trout lakes. Most trout in lakes feed in this shallow water zone. They may be right up in the weedbeds or off on the deeper edges of the weeds or on rocky drop-offs, points, or bays. The medium-sinking line sinks fast enough for use in some deep water as well.

If you can see weedbeds on or near the surface, find some deep pockets or channels in the weeds and fish these carefully. Trout like to cruise into these areas, which are like fish cafeterias. There is lots of food, and they feel safe in the weeds. If you are afraid to put your fly right into the weeds, you won't catch the trout that frequent them. Snagging weeds and having to clean off your fly occasionally are a small price to pay for great trout action.

Where these weedbeds drop off into deeper water is where some of my best fishing has come from. Big trout like the security of deeper water, but they also like the food found in weedbeds. They will cruise the deeper edges and make brief forays into the weeds, many times using them for cover in addition. This means that the shady side of weedbeds often holds the bigger trout.

Slow-sinking (Type I) fly lines are my personal favorite for fishing the shallow flats and weedbeds common in productive trout lakes. These lines sink slowly enough that they do not get too deep, even during a slow retrieve. They are not made for fishing water more than about eight feet deep and do best in one to six feet of water.

A variation of the slow-sink line is the "slime line," a clear fly line that looks like 100-pound-test monofilament but is luckily much softer. This is a great line for fishing over weedy flats in the one to 10-foot range. Some anglers prefer it for spooky fish in flat, shallow water such as beaver ponds. It breaks the surface tension but then sinks slowly. Intermediate fly lines sink even more slowly in skinny water.

Sink-tip lines (five to 17-foot sinking-tips) and sink-head lines (20 to 30-foot sinking-tips) also have their place in nymphing. For years I used an extra-fast, 10-foot sink-tip fly line, and it worked acceptably as long as I fished the four to eight-foot deep water it was suited for. I could usually find some trout interested in my flies at that level. Later I found that full-sinking lines were much more versatile and easy to cast. If you already have a sinking-tip fly line, give it a try.

Some Type I or Type II sink-tips are now available, and they are great when you need a sinking fly line while wading or on the shore. They fish the shallower weedbeds, too, but do not sink to deeper weeds or cruising lanes.

Use leaders two to six feet long for most sinking lines unless longer ones are needed in clear water. Again, divide your hook size by three to find the correct X-rating for your tippet. But tippet rating will still vary greatly, depending on how selective the trout have become. For example, a #8 damselfly-nymph tippet should be about 3X. In really shallow, clear water, however, you might need 4X to get by. On the other hand, a #8 dragonfly nymph is usually taken quite hard, and a 3X-tippet might be too light to hold on a severe take. A 2X in this situation would be more appropriate.

Floating fly lines are great in the shallows, especially in very clear water where a 12 to 20-foot leader is needed. When fish are near the surface feeding on emergers or migrating nymphs, the floater is the best line. It's the one used by anglers stalking visible trout in the shallows.

Stalking visible stillwater trout requires good polarized fishing glasses and the discovery of a good cruising lane where trout cruise shallow. It's like stalking bonefish on the flats. Patience, the ability to spot trout, and a delicate presentation are all musts. I generally prefer weighted nymphs or scuds in size 10 or smaller for this type of fishing.

I often use SIs with floating lines in stillwater. Set up with a long (10 to 15-foot) leader, a relatively small SI, and a small (#18 to #10) weighted nymph. Bead-heads work well. Cast to likely cruising lanes from shore or from watercraft. The retrieve is no retrieve — just let the bug sink. Trout often hit on the drop. When the nymph is deep, start a slow retrieve. Watch the SI for the slightest tap. This is very effective on heavily fished trout lakes because it presents the smaller flies that selective trout like.

With any fly line, you must experiment with retrieves to find which one is acceptable to the trout. When nymphs are used, the retrieves are generally slow. One exception is the dragonfly nymph. The naturals scoot around by squirting water through their body, and they can move pretty fast. The retrieve should be about eight to 12-inch strips at the rate of one a second. Pauses in the retrieve are usually fine, but make several fast strips before pausing one or two counts.

Damselfly nymphs are slow swimmers but very animated, so the retrieve should be short, slow, and jerky. Point the rod right at the fly and wiggle your rod hand quickly as your line hand strips the line in slowly. This creates jiggling motions that simulate the nymphs swimming.

The standard retrieve for most nymphs is a slow, two to 12-inch retrieve with occasional pauses. Just imagine the natural swimming down through the weeds and then try to match the insect's movements. Keeping mental contact with the fly is important. Sometimes the appropriate retrieve is so slow it is almost irritating, but be patient and concentrate on the correct fly speed. When trout want it slow, give it to them that way. Try making one-inch strips, or do the hand-twist method.

It's very important to keep a tight line on slow retrieves. Make sure the wind is not blowing you toward your fly, or slack will develop and you'll miss strikes. One effective retrieve is to troll backwards with your fins, or with the wind, at a very slow pace as you retrieve very slowly. This is also a good search pattern because you will cover a fair piece of water.

Over deeper weedbeds and in weedy channels, use a floating or slow sinking line and a weighted fly. Count down to different depths until you feel the fly in the weeds. Retrieve about five strips. The fly will rise up off the bottom a foot or two. Stop the retrieve and allow the nymph to sink again. Repeat the process.

As with the stillwater SI rig, sometimes the trout hit flies on the sink. As you count down your sinking fly line, keep the line tight and try to feel the light tugs of a trout take. If in doubt, strip the line once or twice. If the line tightens, set the hook. If not, allow it to continue sinking.

OVERLEAF: *A selection of Orvis Muddlers.*

t bank, feel the

athe health and plenty;

see sweet dew-drops kiss

then was... by April

re, hear ...na sing... son...

re, see a blackbird ...

...young,

verock build he...

ive my wear...

se my low...

what po... ...oughts above

ree from ...s love:

ces' cour..., ...and the noise...

I would re...

y Bryan, and a b...

r Sh...

CHAPTER FOUR

CHOOSING THE RIGHT FLY

There was a time when your favorite fly or two were used 80 percent of the time and generally worked. Today, with the number of anglers and the growing numbers of educated trout, you usually need at least a dozen killer nymph patterns in your box to do consistently well in various waters, even if your presentation techniques are impeccable.

Many educated trout have differing habits, even in the same piece of water. Some key in on how naturally their food is presented, some on how accurate their food looks. You must continually adjust the flies and presentation to appeal to the most fish. In most of these locales presentation is the key to success, but fly patterns also make the difference between a slow day and a great day of fishing. The right fly pattern sometimes works even when the presentation is off, as does the right presentation with the wrong fly. But when fish are selective, you need both the right fly and the right presentation for consistent action.

Experimenting with new flies is fun, but most anglers get in a groove. If something is working satisfactorily, they quit experimenting. If you want to gain confidence in new fly patterns, you must use them when fishing is good, not just when you've already tried everything else. One game I like to play is to change a fly after every two fish it catches. This allows you to compare the relative effectiveness of various fly patterns in differing conditions and gives you confidence in many flies. It also often confirms that presentation can be more important than imitation.

When the right fly and the right presentation are needed, changing your flies will indicate that. If you make several changes without success and then go back to your original two-fish catcher with good results, you've found a winner. Remember the time, place, and fly, since you should see the same thing happen next year.

While experimentation is certainly fundamental to nymphing success, changing flies haphazardly and with no firm purpose in mind is usually counterproductive. Once you develop a theory of imitation, you can test it on different waters in different conditions and gradually improve your fly pattern or presentation style.

There is a list of suggested nymph imitations for various water types at the end of this chapter, but I don't believe it's a good idea to tell anglers what one fly to use. Even if you hire a guide and he chooses a fly for you, ask him why he is using that pattern. Learning why you choose a particular fly is more important than just having a fly on that works. Once you know why, not just what, you can use that information in other waters where the situation is similar.

THEORIES OF IMITATION

For years people have been trying to find the magic fly, the one that will always work. There really is no such thing. Everyone has particular flies that have produced in the past. The patterns that work consistently for many anglers in a variety of waters over a period of time become standards and get into the fly boxes of most fly fishermen.

For nymphers, the standards might include the Gold-Ribbed Hare's Ear, Prince Nymph, Muskrat Nymph, Red Fox Squirrel Hair Nymph, Chamois Caddis, Pheasant Tail Nymph, Rubber-Leg Stone, Fur Bug, and Zug Bug. You'll notice that none of these is an exact imitation of anything. They are all suggestive or attractor nymphs. This indicates that the best all-round nymphs are generally not exact hatch-matchers. It also suggests that if you develop your nymphing techniques, these flies or their variations will catch trout anywhere you go.

So why study trout foods and work on exact imitation? When trout get selective, they begin refusing medium-sized or odd-sized foods. When they get selective on small foods, they key in on certain aspects of them. If your fly does not fall within the parameters, it will be rejected. Therefore, specific trout in specific locales at specific times can get super-selective and only accept exact imitations. Each water is different, and you should get some advice from local experts.

Remember that trout have small brains and are unable to analyze all factors of each tidbit of food. Instead, they key on just a few aspects. Attractors may not always have the triggers for selective feeding, but the flies may still trigger curiosity or aggression.

Suggestive flies imitate nothing in particular but many things in general, so they leave the interpretation open to the trout. Curiosity or hunger, both work.

Exact patterns imitate one specific food. Any selective trout not feeding on that exact food will ignore it completely. Trout selectively feeding on that food will be interested.

Not one of the three fly types — attractors, suggestives, and imitators — is better than another, because each can be the best choice in certain situations. Try to decide if you are matching the hatch (exact patterns), searching the water (suggestive patterns), or experimenting with triggers (attractor patterns). Then you will know how to begin choosing a fly.

Matching the hatch is not as exact a science as we might think, because it is only one-third of the equation. Suggestive and attractor patterns also have their place and trout may respond best to those patterns. As I said earlier, matching the hatch is sometimes like force-feeding trout.

Trout perceptions of our flies are also often different than we think. A simple Fur Bug may not look like much to us, but it suggests many food items to the trout. A little dubbing on a #14 hook can be taken by trout as a scud, sow bug, mayfly nymph, small leech, caddis larva, caddis pupa, baby crayfish, small stonefly nymph, riffle beetle larva, cranefly larva, snail, or Snickers bar.

You might put on an exact imitation of a caddis pupa, but if a trout takes it for a cranefly larva or an attractor fly out of curiosity, is it then really an exact imitation? Or if you're fishing in a lake and put on a Prince Nymph, which is generally considered an attractor fly, and the trout takes it for a dragonfly nymph, damselfly nymph, caddis pupa, or minnow, is it then an attractor fly or an exact imitation? Fly categories blend together in the trout's perception. We put the flies into categories, but trout often do no such thing.

What about fly color? There is no doubt that color sometimes makes a difference, yet it would be low on a list of the most important fly attributes. Fly presentation is usually first, fly size is often second, fly shape (in the case of a nymph) or surface impression (with a dry fly) might be third, and color or shade is often last. Many times, trout see a fly pattern as a silhouette, a dark shape against a bright sky.

Conversely, color can be the most important. Egg patterns are often taken by trout feeding on trout or salmon eggs, and when selective, trout will carefully differentiate egg colors. Size or presentation might be more overlooked. Other foods where color is occasionally important are aquatic worms, scuds, sow bugs, stonefly nymphs, and caddis pupae.

The fly's size is important when trout get selective. Uneducated trout often prefer big, flashy flies, but as trout become educated they find that smaller foods are safer to eat. Dry-fly anglers know that if a trout refuses a dry fly, the first thing to do is tie on a smaller imitation. The imprint of the food item on the trout's brain says that the size is wrong, and a smaller fly is often immediately accepted. With nymphs, size is also a factor for selective fish. If you screened a river, found that scuds were the main food available, tried a #12 scud, and still did not get much action, you should try the smaller #16 scud, or even a real small #20 or #22. Because the foods are small, even selective trout must eat lots of them to survive, so your chances increase exponentially as you go down in fly size. A trout may not eat a #12 scud in a day but it might eat 150 #16 scuds and 200 #18s.

At the other end of the spectrum, sometimes extra-large flies get attention. A trout's life hangs in the balance of calories expended and calories ingested. A big food item cannot be ignored, because it represents a major boost to caloric intake. A big stonefly nymph, for example, represents one bite equal to 100 or more bites of small mayfly or midge nymphs. Usually when trout are selective on very small items, enough trout will opportunistically take a large fly to make offering one worth your while. You usually need to cover more water with big flies to find the most opportunistic fish.

Fly shape can also make a big difference. In fast water or murky water, a fly should be a thick, buggy, dark nymph like a Gold-Ribbed Hare's Ear Nymph. If the river slows, a more appropriate pattern might be the thinner Pheasant Tail Nymph. Remember to match fly size to water type for starters, then match fly shape to the water. Slow, clear, spring waters are generally not the place to plunk a #4 stonefly nymph. The appropriate nymph would be a sparsely tied scud, mayfly nymph, or midge, #16 or smaller.

Each fly pattern can be tied differently as well. A scud can be fat with bright colors for fast water, but in shallow, slow water you may want a very pale, thin, translucent pattern. A Gold-Ribbed Hare's Ear Nymph for fast water might be shaped almost like a snail, while the same pattern for slow water might be tied thin and delicate-looking. If you tie your own flies, you have a big advantage. If you don't, you can customize many flies with a sharp pair of scissors.

Many naturals have or display iridescent colors. Peacock herl has long been used to help imitate iridescence. Modern dubbings are starting to be made to imitate the spectrumized colors often displayed by insects, crustaceans, and minnows.

Spectrumized colors are complex colors that become homogenized into one main color. For example, a dubbing that appears brown might not have any brown fibers at all. Spectrumized, it might have orange, green, olive, red, claret, yellow, and black. A nymph tied with this spectrumized color would appear brown from a distance but would reflect subtle variations of many colors as the fly twisted and tumbled with the current. This dubbing simulates life and natural iridescence better than a flat, dyed brown color.

That's one reason natural furs have been used so long for dubbing. Nature seldom creates flat colors. Look closely at a hare's mask (which is used in the Gold-Ribbed Hare's Ear Nymph) and see how many colors were used to make brown. Many of the new synthetic dubbings or blends are made from a mixture of several colors. I like a minimum of three colors in my nymph dubbings, and five is better.

Flash can be a great trigger. Like spectrumized or iridescent colors, flash can suggest life. Attractor flies are often heavily adorned with flash. Flashback nymphs have become popular even for the most selective fish because flash can reflect the natural surroundings just as the natural can, and it can imitate the translucence of a trout food or of the air bubble of many nymphs and pupae. The flash also catches the trout's eye a little more easily. Too much flash in a fly can turn a fish away, but a little seldom hurts and often helps.

Translucence also relates to nymph imitation. In fast, colored water, flies should usually be solid and appear opaque. In slow water, many of a trout's foods are translucent. Smaller foods held up to the light in a clear glass container demonstrate this. Most trout streams or lakes are green-tinted, and when these green surroundings mix with the yellow sunlight, a chartreuse color is produced that shows up in the translucent bodies of insects, crustaceans, and minnows. It's no mistake that many bass lures and flies contain chartreuse. As bright and gaudy as it looks to us, it is a natural color to trout and other gamefish. But it is seldom used for trout.

I frequently add chartreuse to my smaller slow-water, clear-water, or shallow-water flies. I mostly add it to the dubbing, but I've gone as far as tying the whole fly out of chartreuse materials. They all work, even on selective trout. I'm convinced that translucent materials or chartreuse shades imitate the naturals quite well.

Grab several flies and do this experiment. Hold the fly in the light of a table lamp, with a dark background behind the fly. Move the fly back and forth, in and out of the light. If the fly is translucent, you will see the color changing radically as light passes through the materials. Some flies are tied with naturally iridescent fibers like pheasant tail or peacock herl. Notice all the colors they reflect. Your bigger flies will probably be less translucent, but that's okay because fast-water flies are best opaque.

Simple flies like Fur Bugs or scuds are very translucent. I believe that selective trout in slow or clear water often key in on translucence or natural iridescence. I also believe that spectrumization is more important than actual, exact color shades. Just as suggestive flies imitate more than one particular food, spectrumized, translucent, reflective, or iridescent colors on a fly pattern imitate more than one color. The factors mentioned here are much more important than actual fly color. They combine with the shape and size of the pattern and the presentation method to create a realistic, convincing bug to the trout, even if it is not an exact imitation to us.

TYPES OF FLY PATTERNS

In a companion volume in this Library,* top fly-fishing professional Dave Whitlock categorizes all the artificial fly patterns that imitate fish foods as being either *impressionistic, suggestive, imitative,* or *exact imitative.* I have no quarrel with Dave's nomenclature, but when I am dealing exclusively with nymphs, I find it useful to group fly types into only three categories: *attractor, suggestive,* and *imitative.*

Attractors

Attractor nymphs are rarely used, particularly in small sizes (#22 to #16). This may be a mistake. Triggers other than hunger are abundant in attractor flies and often interest trout we assume to be more wary. Attractors attempt to enhance triggers or exploit a trout's weakness for flash or an occasional variation in diet. Extra-large and extra-small attractors are often the key to catching opportunistic trout. Anglers who don't know any better consider attractor flies the domain of beginners or dumb fish and won't use them. Their loss.

Attractors are designed to interact with trout in additional ways besides "trout + food = feeding activity." Basic hunger is only one aspect of a trout's feeding habits. Other elements

---

Fly Fishing for Trout: Volume Four — Imitating and Fishing Natural Fish Foods.

include curiosity, aggression, territoriality, imprinting, faded imprints (or parallels), the Snicker's bar theory, the baseball reaction, and environmental testing. These were covered in my previous book in the Library, *Fly Fishing for Trout: Volume III — Small Fly Techniques.*

The triggers that occur on attractors are flash, iridescence, white, rubber legs, attractor colors, buggy colors, body profile, injured food look, and action or simulated action.

Flash on attractors is common. Tinsel ribbing, flashbacks, flash legs, or reflective dubbing can create something that is very eye-catching. Flash can imitate the sheen of natural insects or the air bubbles they might carry. Because flash also imitates translucence, trout often see flash as natural camouflage. Think about the Schwarzenegger movie *Predator.* The perfect camouflage was a light-bending and reflective suit that blended the predator with the environment. I've tested nymphs made entirely of mylar flash material, and they can work well.

Peacock herl has the natural iridescence that makes it appear life-like or at least intriguing. Trout feeding opportunistically will often take peacock-body nymphs. Use very small peacock-body nymphs for selective trout, and bigger nymphs in fast water or stillwater as productive search patterns.

White on attractors seems to trigger something in trout. White reflects its surroundings, and if the surroundings are moving, as with rivers, the reflections simulate life. White wings on dry flies often create spectacular rises, but white on nymphs works, too. White rubber legs on stonefly nymphs, white wing, or wing cases on Prince Nymphs or Zug Bugs work well. The almost white body of the Chamois Caddis seems to trigger fish occasionally. All white or off-white imitations of stoneflies, mayflies, caddis, scuds, sow bugs, aquatic worms, salmon flesh, minnows, eggs, midges, and craneflies work for some selective trout. Many of the nymphs actually have very light-colored stages when they shed their skins or when they die. Seeing lighter-than-normal bugs is common, so white can be an imitator as well as an attractor. Bleached Pheasant Tail Nymphs and Gold-Ribbed Hare's Ears often work better than the regular models.

Rubber legs are usually considered parts of attractor flies even though the thick rubber imitates the natural legs of stoneflies, crayfish, and the bigger mayflies quite well. The legs twitch and vibrate enticingly. White legs on the Girdle Bug and Bitch Creek Nymph seem to attract trout from deep, swift water. Rubber legs in a variety of colors can be used on nymphs from sizes 10 to 1.

Attractor colors are fluorescent reds, greens, oranges, yellows, and pinks, plus purple. They work well on attractor-type flies during spawning activity, when trout are aggressive, in low-light situations, and in murky water. They are best when blended with dark colors to create contrast. Some of the trout and salmon flies of Alaska are too big and gaudy. For most trout situations, adding a dash of fluorescent color to flies is all that's needed.

Underwater, purple is the closest color to black without being black. Few trout foods are a flat black, and often a purple imitation can trigger a better response than black in stonefly nymphs, leeches, and cased caddis.

Action built into flies can also be a good attractor. Soft marabou tails on flies like Woolly Buggers are enticing. Their subtle movements simulate life well, and their bulk can actually be felt by a trout's lateral-line system when the flies are stripped because they displace water and create low-frequency pressure waves.

Another way to create built-in action is found in a fly I designed called the Wiggle Bug. It is tied from a closed-cell foam and shaped with a diving lip or pressure plate that dives and swims the fly in a serpentine motion when retrieved. Wiggle

Bugs are tied from several inches long — for imitating leeches, minnows, eels, and crayfish — to small sizes that are capable of imitating the swimming motion of damselfly nymphs and small fry or leeches.

The vibrations are felt by the trout, and the trout can find the fly even in dirty water or at night, when vision is worthless for a predator. Although Wiggle Bugs can be made to look like natural foods, they are mostly attractors, and basic attractor colors often outproduce natural colors.

Attractors are designed to trigger something other than hunger in trout, and they are therefore a valuable addition to a nympher's fly arsenal. Use them for aggressive, uneducated trout, but also try them in large and small sizes for opportunistic trout and to trigger something in a trout's head.

Suggestives

Suggestive nymphs are quickly becoming my favorites. The better I get with presentation techniques, the less I find I need to rely on exact imitation to catch trout. I find that they fit into my successful nymph-for-everywhere category very well and accept spectrumized colors with ease.

I'm convinced that they are often seen by trout as better imitations than exact imitations. They are easy to tie, durable, and they catch trout. What more can you ask of a fly? They are the best first choice for unfamiliar waters because they allow you to concentrate on the location of trout and how to present the fly properly and less on perfect imitation (which is difficult even if you know the water).

Suggestive nymphs such as the Gold-Ribbed Hare's Ear, soft-hackle, Teeny Nymph, Carey Special, Pheasant Tail Nymph, Chamois Caddis, March Brown, Red Fox Squirrel Nymph, and Woolly Bugger have stood the test of time and universal

OVERLEAF: *Various ant patterns.*

acceptance. I'd wager that if you have any nymphs in your box, you have at least one of these.

Suggestive flies are accepted by the trout because they look like food but imitate nothing specific, so the trout fits the fly into its perception of what food should look like. It's like an abstract painting that means different things to different people. Suggestive nymphs mean different things to different fish so they may appeal to more trout than exact patterns.

Fishing with suggestive flies will also help you develop your nymphing skills. You can often leave a couple suggestive nymphs on all day, never changing them, just retying the knots after every few fish. You can then concentrate much more on presentation techniques and a lot less on having the right fly. Since presentation is usually more important than imitation, suggestive-nymph anglers often become the most consistent trout catchers around. Day in and day out, throughout the season, they will produce fish consistently.

This does not imply that fly choice isn't important. Often you must experiment with suggestive flies until you find one or two the right size and shape that are consistent producers. Match the fly size and shape to the waters where you fish. Thick, buggy, large flies for fast water and small, translucent, thin flies for slow water and selective trout. A common mistake is staying with one size of fly. You can often get away with a larger fly in the morning or in the early part of the spring or summer, but as fish get more selective, or if they have been fished over for a period, you must go to smaller sizes. Almost all suggestive nymphs can be tied from #2 down to #22. They can be fished in many water types that way.

Suggestive flies are usually best if fished carefully but constantly on the move. Work a piece of water, take a few steps, and work more water. Slow down when you find a concentration of willing trout, and speed up to prospecting speed between productive spots. Fishing upstream is usually best because then you can hook and play the lower trout without disturbing the trout upstream. If you work downstream, you may spook trout downstream with your hooked fish.

Once you get good at nymphing techniques, you will start using suggestive flies much of the time. There are situations where you must go to exact patterns, however.

Exact Imitations

Matching the hatch relates to specific hatches in specific areas at specific times. Exact imitation also includes matching food items other than insects, such as eggs, scuds, and aquatic redworms, almost exactly as we see them.

Once you learn something about the water, you may want to slow down and see how many of the feeding trout you can catch in one small area, instead of just covering the water as you do with suggestive and attractor nymphs. I seldom use this type of fly for searching the water, unless I've already discovered what the trout want and I'm just prospecting for a mother lode. I will use them from drift boats during selective-feeding periods but will almost always combine them with a search (suggestive) pattern.

If you have asked fly shops about local hatches and fly patterns, and have screened the river and compared the samples to your flies, you have a pretty good idea of what to use. Start with some exact nymph imitations fished right along the bottom. I'll usually make one of them a non-insect, like a scud, San Juan Worm, sow bug, or egg pattern. Fishing two of the same nymph is not going to do much for you. Keep changing the one that's not working.

One to two hours before the main hatch of the day, nymphs get active and start drifting. Nymphing can be quite good if you're in the right place and are rigged properly. Fish the faster water coming into a hole or run. Trout will migrate toward the source of the nymphs, usually in riffles and pocket water.

As the hatch gets started, you may see fish flashing under the surface. That indicates it's time to start fishing to suspended trout feeding on nymphs that are rising to the surface. Changing from a straight nymphing rig to a dry-fly indicator rig is often more productive. Make the dry fly an imitation of the adult so the fish can tell you when they are starting to become surface-oriented. When the first trout hits the dry-fly indicator, switch the dropper nymph to an emerging pattern, and you should have some good action on the emerger and dry-fly combo. Toward the end of the emergence, the trout may start preferring dry flies and you can switch to a standard dry-fly rig. I'd bet that you already had enough action on the nymphs and emergers to make a great day. The dry-fly action is just a bonus.

This is a good system for fishing mayfly, caddis, and midge hatches. Things often happen fast once a hatch gets started. I've seen the whole thing finish in a half hour. If you are not ready, you'll spend the whole time rigging up or just trying to figure out what the trout are feeding on. As you might expect, it's not a good time to move much. Fish the area as long as you're getting some action. Once the action slows, and if your car is nearby, you might be able to move upstream a couple miles and repeat the performance if you act quickly. The hatch usually moves upstream fairly quickly but you might be able to hit the head of the action again.

There is usually a lull in the nymphing action right after a hatch. Go to a small suggestive nymph and aim for the small strike zone along the bottom. You'll catch trout that are full but still feeding on bugs drifting within easy reach. On sunny days in summer, the hatches usually take place in the morning or evening. On overcast days, that may change to midday.

Non-insects also have periods of increased activity. Scuds and sow bugs are usually active a couple times a day, and action can be good with them all day long when no other food is more abundant. Before hatches get going, use these types of trout junk food. In the spring, fall, and winter, the most abundant foods available to the trout will often be crustaceans, worms, and eggs.

In the spring or fall, or in the state of Alaska, trout will congregate in spawning areas to feed on eggs and other foods dislodged by spawning activity. Usually 50 to 90 percent of the trout in spawning areas are not spawning but are just hanging around for the omelet buffet.

ADAPTING FLIES

In the last few years, I've tried to tie flies for a specific piece of water, and they generally work better than standard store-bought flies. Something as simple as adding a flashback to your nymph often does the job. Store-bought flies can be adapted to a point, but fly tyers have the advantage, especially with nymphing. Nymphs are inexpensive and generally easy to tie. The variations are endless because each pattern can be modified a dozen different ways.

Adaptations from the Vise

Bead-head nymphs have been popular in Europe for some time and Americans are catching on in a big way. Almost any nymph can be changed by adding a bead head. Why do bead heads work? Bead heads are metal or glass that add weight at the head and allow the fly to ride more level. A hook's bend is heavy, and when this is combined with the resistance of the water on the leader, nymphs often ride nose up. The bead helps the fly remain level, improving the drift. It also helps overcome presentation flaws by getting the fly into the strike zone more often. The flash may also catch the trout's eye and look like a nymph's air bubble.

I've been putting a dot of fluorescent yellow or orange T-shirt paint on the backs of some small nymphs. The attractor color seems to trigger a trout's curiosity in addition to making it stand out among the other foods drifting by.

Try using materials that are colored differently than normal. I often tie little purple, orange, chartreuse, and cream Pheasant Tail Nymphs. The odd colors work surprisingly well on trout rejecting the standard brown Pheasant Tail Nymph.

Flash can be used in a number of ways. Try a small nymph with three strands of Crystal Flash tied for a tail. Try a flashback in silver, pearlescent, or green. The flashback looks like the mayfly nymphs that are getting ready to hatch. Use them just before the daily mayfly emergence.

Twist a couple strands of flash with your caddis larva or midge dubbing. When it is wrapped in this way, the subtle flash looks like natural movement and translucence. Dubbing loose over tinsel chenille will do something similar for imitating the thick body of a cased caddis and the bits of mica that are stuck to the case.

Floating nymphs and emergers can be improved by adding some Antron or synthetic yarn as a trailing shuck or wing case. A marabou fluff tail will add action.

As the fly is being tied, ask yourself what type of water it will be fished in and what shape the nymph should be for that water. In general, you should already know that bulky flies are ideal for fast water and that slow water dictates sparse, delicate flies.

Substitution of materials or colors leads to many variations of each pattern. Why the variations? Because if the trout keep seeing the same things, they will become conditioned to rejecting them automatically. Something more natural or interesting will elicit responses from trout. I'm continually amazed at how quickly trout can get used to fly patterns. It only takes a few bad drifts for trout to become suspicious. Change to a slightly different fly and do a good drift, and the trout is often yours. Many days I have stood in the same place changing flies every two fish and catching trout after trout.

Onstream Customization

Every angler should carry a pair of needle-nose scissors onstream. They can adapt and improve your standard nymphs in many ways. The scissor tips can pick out dubbing for a buggier thorax or more legs on a scud pattern.

Sometimes less is more. Nymphs which are buggy are good for fast water but too bulky for slow water. Pick the dubbing out and then trim the long fibers — sort of a nymph haircut and a thinning. The hook part of Velcro also picks the dubbing out nicely. Your fishing vest or jacket probably has some Velcro built in.

I find that some flies, especially store-bought flies, will get really shaggy after being fished with for a short period of time. In fast water this is fine, but in slow water it looks ridiculous. I find that scuds, dubbed stonefly nymphs, and cranefly larvae that are kept trimmed produce better than their shaggy counterparts.

Most store-bought flies come with too much hackle for legs. Remember that nymphs, like all insects, have only six legs, not 96. The tails often have the same problem — just too many. Especially when fishing for selective trout, leave only two or three tail fibers. Commercial Woolly Buggers have too bulky a tail, almost guaranteed. Trim about half the fibers off.

Conversely, sometimes a used fly will lose its tails and stop working. A good example is the Pheasant Tail Nymph. Too many tails are no good, but no tails will interest few trout if they are feeding on mayfly nymphs.

If trout are feeding on midges, which have no tails, and you run out of midges, just cut the tails off small mayfly nymphs and give them an instant species change.

Choosing the right fly has too often been a matter of para-
noia or superstition. Following is a basic formula to narrow
down your choices to a small selection of nymphs that will
work in the water where you fish. The flies recommended will
just be a place to start and will depend on the natural foods
available. Take a screen sample to find out more specifics, and
ask fly shops about local patterns.

Most of the flies recommended are the same as the patterns
sold in popular fly-tackle catalogs and in fly shops, although
some may vary. Use small patterns for selective trout and larger
patterns for "easy" fish. Most of the patterns can be modified
by trimming or adding bead heads, flashbacks, and other fea-
tures. The variations are endless, but these tables should give
you a good place to start for various waters.

NYMPH PATTERNS FOR RIVERS

SLOW OR SHALLOW WATERS AND SPRING CREEKS

Pattern Size	Pattern
#20 to #14	Antron Nymph
#22 to #14	A.P. Nymph
#24 to #16	Brassie
#20 to #14	Fur Bug
#18 to #14	Harrop CDC Emerger
#20 to #14	Harrop Floating Nymph
#16 to #12	LaFontaine Emergent Caddis Pupa
#18 to #10	Light Cahill
#18 to #12	mayfly emerger
#22 to #14	midge larva

#22 to #14	scud
#18 to #14	Serendipity
#18 to #14	Skip Nymph
#20 to #14	sunken terrestrials
	(ants, beetles, hoppers, etc.)
#20 to #14	Trueblood Otter Nymph
#26 to #16	WD-40 Nymph

MODERATE CURRENTS, RIFFLES, AND RUNS

#20 to #12	Brassie
#14 to #10	caddis larva
#18 to #12	Chamois Caddis
#8 to #4	cranefly larva
#10	egg
#16 to #12	Floating Nymph
#18 to #10	Fur Bug
#16 to #10	Gold-Ribbed Hare's Ear
#16 to #8	Halfback
#16 to #12	LaFontaine Sparkle Caddis Pupa
#22 to #16	Palomino Nymph
#16 to #10	Peeking Caddis
#16 to #12	Pheasant Tail Nymph
#16 to #8	Prince Nymph
#10	San Juan Worm
#16 to #12	Scintillator
#20 to #12	scud
#16 to #10	soft-hackle
#16 to #6	sunken terrestrials
#6 to #2	Wiggle Bug

#10 to #4	Bird's Nest
#10 to #2	Bitch Creek Nymph
#8 to #2	cranefly larva
#10 to #6	Golden Stone
#12 to #8	Prince Nymph
#12 to #6	Red Fox Squirrel Nymph
#10 to #2	Rubber-Leg Stone
#8	San Juan Worm
#10 to #2	Simulator
#14 to #4	Teeny Nymph
#2	Wiggle Bug
#8 to #2	Woolly Bugger
#10 to #4	Yuk Bug

ALASKA

#8	Bead Egg
#10 to #6	Bird's Nest
#8 to #2	Bitch Creek Nymph
#8 to #2	Egg-Sucking Leech
#14 to #8	Flashback Pheasant Tail
#10 to #2	flesh fly
#10 to #6	fry
#8	Glo-Bug
#10	Iliamna Pinkie
#8 to #4	Lead-Eye Egg Leech
#14 to #10	maggot
#2	Wiggle Bug
#8 to #2	Woolly Bugger

NYMPH PATTERNS FOR LAKES

OPEN WATER AND ROCKY BOTTOMS

Pattern Size	*Pattern*
#12 to #10	caddis larva
#10 to #2	Canadian Blood Leech
#12 to #4	Carey Special
#10 to #2	crayfish
#14 to #8	Halfback
#8 to #4	Marabou Leech
#12 to #6	Renegade
#14 to #8	scud
#10	snail
#6 to #2	Wiggle Leech
#10 to #2	Woolly Bugger
#12 to #8	Zug Bug

WEEDY AND SHALLOW AREAS

#10	backswimmer
#18 to #10	Blood Midge
#10 to #4	Canadian Brown Leech
#12 to #8	damselfly nymph
#8 to #4	dragonfly nymph
#12 to #8	Peacock Wooly Worm
#14 to #8	Prince Nymph
#14 to #10	scud
#14 to #10	sow bug
#14 to #10	Trueblood Otter Nymph
#10	water boatman
#8	Wiggle Damsel

#14 to #10	caddis larva
#12 to #10	damselfly nymph
#12	egg
#16 to #10	mosquito larva
#16 to #8	Muskrat Nymph
#16 to #10	scud
#18 to #12	Serendipity
#16 to #12	Siberian Wood Ant
#16 to #10	soft-hackle
#16 to #10	Tellico Nymph
#16 to #12	Timberline Emerger
#10 to #6	Woolly Bugger
#12 to #8	Zug Bug

CONCLUSION

Tying everything in this book together may take you a while. Just take it one aspect at a time and refer back to it often. Soon you will see how it all ties together and will begin to do embarrassingly well in many situations.

We've learned about the foods trout feed on, how trout interact with their foods, and how to imitate and fish the imitations. When you understand the principles and adapt them to your waters, you will begin to see trout water everywhere in a different light. You'll be able to look at a piece of water and already have a good idea of what nymphing style and pattern will work there.

One thing that brings me a lot of joy is teaching others how to nymph and watching them light up as they begin to catch trout with my methods. I guided for more than nine years and was able to introduce many people to nymphing, and many of the ideas I've presented here came from developing ways to teach my clients and friends. One of the great things about this sport is that you never quit learning unless you choose to.

Teaching can also be frustrating because some anglers simply have a mental block about subsurface flies. Nymphs cannot be fished exactly like dry flies. Most anglers can do okay with dry flies because presentation is relatively easy. A nymphing technique can be learned in a day, but nymphing in general is much more demanding of skill than dry-fly fishing and takes a lifetime to perfect. Be patient, and challenge yourself to learn something new each time you fish.

Some of my most exciting experiences in fly fishing have come from sight-nymphing to large trout or nymphing a piece of deep, swift water correctly and hooking a monster trout. It may also come from catching a good trout from deep, fast water or a small trout from clear, shallow spring water. Nymphing has something for everyone. Successfully presenting a scud, egg, or nymph to a big trout is a very satisfying experience. So is using a light rod and small attractor nymphs for little stream trout that seldom exceed 12 inches.

When you get into the right groove and everything comes together, you can catch and release trout all day and have a great time. When you get into the place where you can catch lots of trout, you also get into the place where you have an increased responsibility to protect the resource.

Catch-and-release has been around long enough to prove its worth. As Lee Wulff said, "A trout is too valuable a resource to be caught just once." His statement rings even truer today. The number of people on trout waters is increasing, and all anglers must do their part.

During the five years I guided on the Green River in Utah, I told clients that despite the high densities of trout found in that river, if every angler that fished the river in a year kept only one fish, there would be no fish left in the river by the end of the year. That is true in many waters now. If you have a desire to keep trout, there is nothing wrong with that if the law allows, but do so responsibly. Wild fish and river trout are too valuable and should be left where they are. There are plenty of stocked lakes where put-and-take is the management principle and keeping a couple planters won't hurt much.

Learn how to release trout properly. With every trout caught, try to improve your technique for releasing trout unharmed. I've always believed that when you get a lot from something, you should also give a lot back. Get involved with local conservation battles and lend support to the clubs and organizations that help preserve the integrity of watersheds in your area. Water is a barometer of the overall health of an ecosystem. Don't get caught up in battling other outdoor-user groups. They should be your allies for protecting the resource and environs.

Nymphing has become a passion for me because I can interact with nature in so many situations and I have the opportunity to relax and experience re-creation. Nature has been touched by the hand of God, and when we involve ourselves in something so close to something so special, our minds are opened up and our souls expanded. I've never met a person who could fish and worry at the same time. I've also seldom met anyone that loves life more than a fly fisher. Life in a city can close off parts of us that only immersing ourselves in nature for a time can overcome. When that part of us is open, we feel much more complete and happy. I believe that interaction with nature is an important part of who we are.

Fly fishing gives us sort of a divine air, like we are part of a select group that knows something others don't. To some, it becomes a snobbery and can damage the perceived image and support from others. If we instead take our stewardship to the environment seriously, we will be more teachable and will also have the desire to teach others instead of separate ourselves from them or put ourselves above them.

I believe that fishing and life in general should be seen from a holistic view. That is why I don't believe in telling someone to stand on a particular rock on a specific run and cast 30 feet, mend twice, and let their off-pink #17 1/2 Hendrickson Nymph drift over a specific rock to catch a specific trout. I want to teach you the principles and let you think and govern your fly fishing for yourself.

Start thinking subsurface and pretty soon you will begin to visualize a world that is different from the one we live in. Like a virtual-reality program that is installed in our minds, if we can see it in our mind's eye, we can nymph it properly, with an intensity we've not experienced before. There is something intriguing and refreshing about water. Learning how to nymph is one way for us to come closer to the thing that gives us life and joy.

Give nymphing a try, and lose yourself for a little while in the environs of the aqueous world. Have fun experimenting with flies, presentation techniques, theories of imitation, and water types. Nymphing is one of those endeavors that can get into your psyche and become a part of who you are. Tight lines always.

INDEX